Play and Practice in the Early Years Foundation Stage

Play and Practice in the Early Years Foundation Stage

Edited by
Natalie Canning

Los Angeles | London | New Delhi
Singapore | Washington DC

First published 2011

SAGE Publications Ltd
1 Oliver's Yard
55 City Road
London EC1Y 1SP

SAGE Publications Inc.
2455 Teller Road
Thousand Oaks, California 91320

SAGE Publications India Pvt Ltd
B 1/I 1 Mohan Cooperative Industrial Area
Mathura Road
New Delhi 110 044

SAGE Publications Asia-Pacific Pte Ltd
33 Pekin Street #02–01
Far East Square
Singapore 048763

Library of Congress Control Number: 2010922894

British Library Cataloguing in Publication data
A catalogue record for this book is available from the British
Library

ISBN 978–1-84860–996-9
ISBN 978–1-84860–997-6 (pbk)

Typeset by Dorwyn, Wells, Somerset
Printed in Great Britain by the MPG Books Group
Printed on paper from sustainable resources

Contents

Acknowledgements

I would like to acknowledge the work of all contributors to the text and the practitioners who have welcomed me into their settings and taken time to provide me with insights into their practice. I appreciate the time colleagues and early years professionals have taken in supporting me with the structure and content of this book, in particular Sue and Mandy for their wise words and commitment to play, Karen for her weekly telephone calls of encouragement and unwavering belief in me, and Mike for his endless support, always being on the end of a phone or email and keeping me on track. I would especially like to acknowledge Juliet Doswell for being my critical reader and for her constantly positive outlook and support, and Rachel Appleby for access to her dissertation on creativity. Thanks must also go to Jo, her team, and all the parents at Farm Days for allowing me to spend time observing and playing, and finally to Jude Bowen and Amy Jarrold at SAGE for their support and assistance throughout this project.

Case Studies

The case studies included in this publication are a composite of numerous children in various settings, compiled over the authors' many years of experience, and are not specific to any one child, practitioner or setting.

About the Editor
and Contributors

Editor

Natalie Canning is a Lecturer in Education – Early Years at The Open University. Her background is in playwork and social work, particularly in supporting children to explore personal, social and emotional issues through play. She has published a number of articles relating to professional development and the early years and has presented at national and European conferences. Her main research is in the area of children's empowerment in play and she is currently involved in research on developing children as autonomous learners. She has taught across a variety of Early Childhood undergraduate and postgraduate programmes.

Contributors

Mandy Andrews is a Senior Lecturer at the University of Worcester in the Centre for Early Childhood within the Institute of Education. She teaches on Early Years Professional Status routes and undergraduate and postgraduate modules in Early Childhood. She was formerly Project Director of a large SureStart Local Programme and Children's Centre in Cornwall. Her research interests include leadership and children's play and empowerment.

Karen Appleby has a professional heritage in early years teaching. She is a Senior Lecturer in Early Childhood and Learning and Teaching Fellow at the University of Worcester. She is Partnership Co-ordinator for the Centre for Early Childhood, in the Institute of Education, and teaches across a variety of Early Childhood programmes. Previously she has worked as the Course Leader for the BA (Hons) Integrated Early Childhood Studies and HND in Early Childhood Studies.

Sue Callan is an Associate Lecturer in Education – Early Years at The

Open University. She is a former Senior Lecturer in the Centre for Early Childhood at the University of Worcester, where she worked with students on Sector Endorsed Foundation Degrees in Early Years, BA (Hons) Early Childhood Studies and those seeking Early Years Professional Status. Sue's background is in community pre-schools and playwork with considerable experience of delivering vocational courses. She is a contributor to *Mentoring in the Early Years* and *Reflective Practice in the Early Years* and co-editor of *Managing Early Years Settings – Leading and Supporting Teams,* all published by SAGE.

Carole Ellis is a Family Support Worker with Herefordshire County Council. She is based in a Children's Centre in South Herefordshire. In her role as part of a multi-professional team supporting community development and family engagement with local services, Carole uses a play-based approach to support children and their families. She is an experienced practitioner with a background as a nursery nurse and senior teaching assistant, supporting children through play for more than twenty two years. Carole has contributed to research in developing practice in working with fathers groups, as part of her Sector Endorsed Foundation Degree in Early Years.

Michael Reed has a career that has involved senior positions in schools, developing and managing a large day nursery, and running a training and development consultancy. He has worked on projects for The Open University forming part of the course development and writing team for the Foundation Degree and written for a number of publications. He teaches on a range of undergraduate and postgraduate early years programmes at the University of Worcester as part of the Centre for Early Childhood tutorial team.

Helen Richards has worked as a NNEB nursery nurse since 1977 and has also worked with children and young people from birth to nineteen years in mainstream and special education schools and the voluntary sector. She is dedicated to inclusive practice, which is intrinsic to her role working with families in the community as a Support for Families Worker specialising in Play and Portage at North Herefordshire Children's Centre. Helen has a Sector Endorsed Foundation Degree in Early Years and her research interests include increasing public awareness of the importance of early years and the development of the children's workforce.

Rosie Walker is a Social Worker by training who has worked in a variety of childcare settings, including Social Care, Child Guidance, the NSPCC and Child Protection Training. She has acted as a Guardian ad Litem and set up a Family Support Service, as well as being an Associate Tutor on the NPQICL course for two years. For the last seven years she has managed two Phase 1 Children's Centres and has recently taken a new post as a Senior Lecturer in the Centre for Early Childhood at University of Worcester.

List of Continuous Professional Development (CPD) Activities

List of Tables and Figures

Tables

Figures

Introduction

Natalie Canning

This book takes the perspective that play is fundamental to every interaction and connection children make. It argues that play should form
the basis and be at the forefront of early years practice as children are
experts in their own experiences and interests and they use play as a
way in which to explore and experiment with emotions, social interactions, new ideas and learning. In England the Early Years Foundation
Stage (EYFS) underpins practice with children from birth to five years of
age. The premise of this book is to support practitioners working with
the EYFS to develop their knowledge, understanding, reflection and
analysis on how play can be central to practice and underpin everything they do with children. Consequently the book has several
interrelated themes which permeate the chapters.

It analyses children's play from a 'can do' perspective, considering
that in play the possibilities are endless and only limited by the
boundaries of an adult world. To embrace this perspective means
that as a practitioner you will be asked to consider how you can trust
children in play to make their own decisions, take risks and attempt
challenges that push your boundaries as well as extending children's
experiences. The book argues for autonomy and freedom in child-
initiated play where you can observe play to identify children's
interests and use these for future planning. Play is seen in the context of holistic development and as such the chapters ask you to
consider the impact of play opportunities in developing children's
curiosity, experimenting and risk taking and the flexibility of
resources, time and space in exploring new ideas.

The way in which you facilitate play is another central theme. This
will require you to reflect and consider your own values about play,
learning and development and how they match or identify tensions
with the content of the EYFS. In exploring such values you will also
be asked to consider the balance between child-initiated and more
structured activities that are provided in your setting and how they

1

impact on the way in which you interpret and apply the EYFS in practice. Consequently observation, assessment and planning will feature in all of the chapters as part of supporting holistic development through play, but also in order to recognise that play is not linear or compartmentalised but a motivating factor for children's engagement and participation.

The book is organised around the four principles of the EYFS and the chapters within each of the four sections offer different theoretical perspectives of play underpinning practice in the context of supporting the development of a unique child, positive relationships, enabling environments and learning and development. Each principle is illustrated with a case study from practice. These form an integral part to the chapters and sections of the book and are used not only to reveal the complexities of play but also to provide practical examples to support theory in practice. Practitioners' views are reflected and the child's voice is also a central aspect in analysing the case studies. Through these the practicalities of observation, assessment and planning are explored, reflecting the diverse ways these can be implemented in practitioners' experiences as well as in the context of the settings represented.

Throughout the chapters children's experiences in play are examined, advocating for child-initiated play which reflects a core value of the book. Each chapter asks you to reflect critically on your own values and beliefs about play through a continuous professional development (CPD) activity, based on the arguments presented within the text for each chapter. Consequently the book asks you to consider how your values about play affect your practice and interaction with children. The CPD activities are designed so that you can use them as part of team meetings or staff development, or if you are a tutor or local authority officer for training or teaching activities. Their purpose is to help you further understand and analyse the ambiguity of providing opportunities for play in practice and what the implications are for your particular situation, setting or context.

Although the book is centred on play and practice in the EYFS it is not solely about implementing policy. However policy – in the form of the practice guidance and statutory framework – does underpin the book's content. This is to support you in interpreting play to formulate your own perspective about the importance of play as part of a child's social world. Play is central to facilitating children's personal wellbeing and the book argues that children should be able to control the intent of their own play to support the exploration of who they are.

Section 1

A Unique Child

'A unique child recognises that every child is a competent learner from birth who can be resilient, capable, confident and self-assured. The commitments are focused around development, inclusion, safety and health and well being.' (DCSF, 2008f: 9)

A Unique Child

📁 Case Study: Playing with Cardboard Boxes

Natalie Canning

The children in this case study are aged between three and a half and five years old. It is based on a non-participant narrative observation of play in a preschool.

Cherry is the manager of a preschool in a church hall which means that all of the equipment has to be brought out and packed away at the end of each session. Recently she has noticed that the children have become predictable in relation to their play choices and she wants to make a few changes. With the support of her staff and over a period of a few weeks she has collected a range of cardboard boxes that differ in size and large cardboard tubes. She was lucky that one of her staff had just bought a new fridgefreezer so they could provide one really large box. Cherry planned the morning session so that when the children arrived there would be nothing in the hall apart from the cardboard boxes. The staff agreed that they would not suggest to the children what to do with the boxes or become involved in the play, unless they were specifically asked to take on a role or if the play became dangerous.

The children came into the play space and at first did not know what to do. They looked expectantly at the practitioners who initially busied themselves with other matters so that the children had time to figure out what they should do without looking to an adult for support. Some of the older children took the lead and started to move a few of the boxes that had been piled up. The biggest box was at the back of the pile so Michael opened one end and crawled inside. More children started to join in, some taking boxes off to the side of the room and playing their own imaginary game, and others putting boxes on top of each other to see how high they could go before they fell down. Eva was one of these children. She collected some of the smaller boxes and took them to one side of the room and began to build a tower. When it reached a certain height the tower started to lean and eventually fell over. Eva repeated this process again and again. She started to become frustrated, kicking one of the boxes. Shona came over and helped her begin to build the tower again. She put two of the boxes together on the floor to make a base and then proceeded to build the tower. Eva was pleased that they could build to a greater height before it finally lost its balance and collapsed to the floor.

James stayed on the fringes of the play, hoping to be invited in by the other children. He has a speech delay and usually has Sarah, his key worker, nearby to support him. He looked around the play space, picked up a spare cardboard box and went across to Peter who was playing to one side of the main game. James offered the box to Peter who looked like he was making a car out of one of the boxes. Peter shook his head and proceeded to ignore James. James backed away from him and seeing that William was now watching, James moved towards him and other children who were organising themselves to start a new game. William then put the cardboard box that James was holding onto James's head, which gave him a signal that he could join in the game.

A few of the other children put smaller boxes on their heads and ran around the room pretending to be firemen, making a 'ne-nar' sound. A commotion broke out when Michael, who had claimed the largest box as his 'den', was invaded by the children who were firemen. They quickly turned into pirates, complete with newly identified pirate helmets, to claim their 'ship'. A series of battle lines were then drawn, with the children who had been building towers now offering to build a defence wall to keep the pirates out. The game brought all of the children together, with each of them taking on a role and participating in the play, and eventually with Michael's den being 'captured' and turned into a pirate ship. Michael, who was a confident and vocal child, expressed his anger at this and was slightly disconcerted by so many children descending into his space. Daniel saw Michael's dismay and patted him on the arm saying, 'don't worry, play with me'. Michael, recovering from the initial shock of his 'den' being taken away, shouted to the others that if it was going to be a ship then he should be captain. The children, busy with their other roles, ignored this demand and did not really object. Apart from the noise level rising by a considerable amount, the play evolved naturally and the practitioners were not asked to join in. Neither did they need to intervene as minor conflicts seemed to reach a natural resolution.

1

Identifying Unique Qualities in Play

Natalie Canning

Chapter Objectives

This chapter locates the child at the centre of play and practice and analyses the concept of play as an intrinsic motivator for children to initiate and develop play opportunities. It explores why play is so difficult to define and how this impacts upon practitioners' ability to provide children with opportunities to express their 'unique qualities'. It also examines the EYFS in terms of 'a unique child', specifically emotional, social and spiritual development and how this translates into interpretive and subjective practice.

What is play?

The term 'play' has been used and interpreted in many ways in the early years. The pioneers of play, such as Froebel (1782–1852), McMillan (1860–1931), Isaacs (1885–1948), Steiner (1861–1925) and Piaget (1896–1980), placed an emphasis on different elements of play depending on their research interests and experiences, and over the last ten years there have been significant contributions from researchers on the implications for play and practice. What they have said about children's play has influenced what practitioners believe and do in practice. Researching different perspectives about play not only helps practitioners to develop a view about its importance as part of a child's social world, but also supports practitioners in becoming aware of the value of play to build up children's interests, explorations, curiosity and skills. However, the challenge inherent in the term 'play' is that it is often misinterpreted by practitioners within the same setting let alone within the wider early years community. How one person defines play may conflict with someone else's view, but more often than not there will be subtle differences in what practitioners believe about what constitutes a play experience. This in turn contributes to what Sutton Smith (1997) describes as the ambiguity of play, where the diverse nature of play means that it is interpreted differently and is difficult to define.

A particular view of play may be promoted in your setting which as a result influences your practice in how it is organised, the resources you provide, and the general ethos of the setting. This is significant when applied to the EYFS because the documentation refers to 'play as underpinning practice' (DCSF, 2008e: 7) but is less clear on what this means in practice or how it may be achieved. The majority of practitioners will observe what children are interested in, plan a series of activities, record the outcomes, and then assess the children's progress. This is a clear procedural format, but when the scale of control is tipped in the favour of the practitioner the child's autonomy may be marginalised, with play then becoming something that is organised around the child rather than emerging from their own explorations. The following examples are from a range of settings that have been described by practitioners as play:

- children making identical 'Father Christmas' faces from specified craft material supplied by the practitioners;

- children having a choice of four tables with different materials on them (such as plasticine, Lego, sand and crayons) where they are not allowed to transfer items to different tables and there is a limit on the time that can be spent on each table;

- children being asked by a practitioner to count the number of cups and plates they have laid out whilst in the middle of a 'tea party' role play.

These examples illustrate the way in which play can sometimes be seen as a set of 'activities' with measurable learning outcomes. They do not however place the child at the centre of the process, as each is led by the nature of the environment, the final outcome, or the value a practitioner places on the content of an activity. To reflect a more child-centred ethos, Skills Active (2004) suggest that play

Smith et al. (2003: 183) suggest that children can understand other people's emotions, desires and beliefs by around three to four years of age, but also that there are important precursors for children to be able to understand what another person may be experiencing. These consist of:

- self-awareness where the child knows what they are doing in play and what the consequences may be;

- the capacity for pretence and to suspend 'real world' events;

- being able to distinguish reality from pretence.

Children's natural disposition towards self-motivated play stimulates these skills, for example, using a cardboard box 'as if' it was a shield to protect them from pirates. In pretend play children are able to conjure up characters with emotions and desires of their own. This reflects, to some extent, part of their own feelings as they project this into their play to test out or rehearse different emotions and responses from others. In self-directed play children will naturally involve emotions into the play. They will watch each other's reactions, and, at around four years old, can take account of someone's actions and from this predict their emotional state (Smith et al., 2003). For example, in the case study the children were aware of Michael's anger on finding that his den had been commandeered as a pirate ship and were also sympathetic to his rather demanding request that he must then become the captain of the ship.

Emotional development has also been defined by Thoits (1989: 318) who highlighted three components which contribute to emerging unique qualities. She has argued that emotional responses can consist of one or a combination of these and here these are related to children's play:

- *children's ability to appraise a play situation or context*; for example when Michael found the biggest box, opened it up and crawled inside;

- *their ability to understand a physiological sensation*; for example when talking to the children after the play in the case study they were able to describe their feelings of uncertainty and being a little scared when they first came into the preschool, as their normal environment had been changed to include a pile of cardboard boxes;

- *their ability to display expressive gestures*; for example when in the case study Eva showed her frustration by kicking the boxes when they fell down after making a tower.

Demonstrating this type of emotional response in play is just one dimension of 'a unique child'. Whalen (1995) has identified another important aspect in exploring a child's sense of who they are and considering the fine detail of children's social worlds. She has suggested that the interactional richness children acquire in social situations is essential to their development. When children play with others they learn social rules and gain an opportunity to practise what they have learnt in their immediate home environment. When children enter into role play, for example, there is usually much discussion about who is going to take on the main characters: this is very clear in the case study, with a large amount of negotiation being undertaken to decide on the role of 'captain', 'head pirate' and 'parrot'. Play can also teach some tough lessons when dominant characters (in this case Michael) usually seem to get their own way. He managed this through being physical with the boxes, making the first move on the largest box, and not being afraid to voice his opinion. Fabes et al. (2003) identified this play as active forceful play that can help children establish a hierarchical pecking order and then use this position to direct the play to their own advantage. Only when the majority of the group 'ganged up' on Michael did the dynamics of the play change, yet he was quickly able to re-establish himself by seeking peer support from Daniel. This demonstrates the detailed way in which children will first initiate, then organise and accomplish play as a socially shared experience. This fine balance of collaborative interactions is dependent upon the children in the play situation using their individual qualities to contribute and extend imaginative play. The children were not aware that they were practising and extending their capabilities, but the practitioners were able to record significant examples to build on their evidence for 'a unique child'.

Personal, Social and Emotional Development (PSED)

The overarching message of the PSED element of the EYFS is that children should have experiences where they can explore who they are and can interact with others. The cardboard box play provided an ideal opportunity for the children to display high levels of engagement that were personally directed by the choices they made. The open-ended nature of the play ensured that there was not a preconceived outcome and using observation practitioners were able to examine what individual children did with the boxes. Cherry, the preschool manager, noted:

> Eva was very interesting to observe; usually in more structured play she would have given up on building the tower when it fell down. Although she displayed her frustration she stuck with it, which really showed a more determined side to her. (Interview, May 2009)

In the case study the cardboard boxes facilitated the children's ability to be creative and immerse themselves in imaginative play. They were able to adapt their game and follow their own play needs, but also play collaboratively when they come together as a group. The children demonstrated their capacity to express themselves individually (with outbursts from Michael and Eva), while others demonstrated an understanding of what was required on a practical and emotional level to help their friends in the play (Daniel and Shona). The way in which the children interacted with each other demonstrated how they were able to assess the situation and have an understanding of each other's needs. Bauman and May (2001) have suggested that children gain a sense of power by having the autonomy to make play decisions and respond to their peers' emotional needs. They argue that having a sense of power in play provides children with the capacity to develop emotionally and socially. The relationship between Daniel and Michael in the case study demonstrates how Michael maintains his sense of control over the play, but how Daniel facilitates this through his ability to understand and empathise in the situation. These actions support both boys' self-confidence and self-esteem.

Spiritual development

It is important to recognise that these observations are subjective as they are based on the prior knowledge and understanding the practitioners had of the children's personalities and their experiences. Therefore, it is essential not to underestimate the knowledge you possess about the children in your care. It is important to discuss with colleagues how you interpret and apply the principles and six areas of learning of the EYFS within your practice. For example, within the PSED area of learning and development the EYFS recommends that you 'plan activities that promote emotional, moral, spiritual and social development together with intellectual development' (DCSF, 2008e: 25). At first glance this seems straightforward, however, there are perhaps further questions to ask based on your knowledge, understanding and interpretation of children's play:

- What do you believe supports development? Are you supporting or directing play? Are you providing opportunities to explore or deciding upon ways that could be seen as controlling how, when and why children play?

- Are you and your colleagues clear about what is meant by spiritual development?

- Do you believe that all activities should contain these elements and how easy is it to incorporate this into your practice?

It is important to discuss these types of questions with your colleagues in order to have a united approach when working with children so they can receive consistent responses to support their development. For example, spiritual development is something that is highly subjective and can be interpreted in many different ways. Hyde (2008) states that the underlying factor of spiritual development is listening to children's voices, something that you may consider you do on a daily basis. However, how do you safeguard against implementing your own perceptions on what children choose to engage in and how do you know that what they choose to do is actually providing them with opportunities to develop their intuitive or spiritual capacities?

A child-centred approach

One way to investigate this is to use the Mosaic Approach with children (Clark and Moss, 2001). Allowing children to use different mediums (such as taking pictures, making a video, or taking you on a tour of their play space) where they have the autonomy to express their interests and explore their emotions can provide an insight into how they experience and perceive their environment. This not only allows you to evaluate how the opportunities you provide for them are received, but also offers an insight into what children value. However, as professionals you need to be open to 'hearing' what children are saying and to also be prepared for the fact that they may not see the setting in the same way you do. Children see their play differently to adults as it is they who are immersed in the fantasy, role play, rough and tumble, outside play, etc. You may observe and record your interpretation of the play, but only the children involved in that play will know the motivation for wanting to do whatever they are engaged in. Children who feel safe and secure enough to share their perceptions and experiences will often offer more personal reflections, for example positive and negative comments about their play environment or playmates. This can be a valuable resource to inform future planning for positive play opportunities.

The value children place on play stems from cultural influences where children link their play experiences to their family, their immediate play environment, and the wider community to which they belong. Play is something that happens in all cultures, although it may be organised in different ways and also be dependent on the play environment. Hyder (2005: 21) recognises that 'all children in all societies appear to engage in activities which would fulfil some of the criteria of play'. He defines this as children exploring and pretending as a mechanism for engaging with the world. This also provides a commonality of bringing children together and contributing to their sense of belonging (Royal College of Psychiatrists, 2006). This is not always an easy process and children can feel rejected and frustrated at not being able to be fully part of the game. It is evident that in the case study James may have had a similar experience. He chose to stay on the periphery of the play for some time, not sure how to enter into the game with the others. He attempted to make contact with Peter who was playing to one side of the main action, but was rejected by him. He then moved around to the other side of the play space and was finally able to join in with the 'pirate' game as the different groups of children joined together in a common aim of capturing the 'ship'.

Key person

The EYFS, by incorporating the role of the Key Person into how you design your practice, has underpinned the value and importance of continuity, progression and security for the child. The Key Person is an essential link between home and the early years setting. This was exemplified in the case study through Sarah, James's key person. She has worked with James for six months and admitted that she wanted to 'rescue' him when she saw how he was struggling to mix with the other children. James has delayed speech and because of this finds it difficult to communicate and make his needs known to other children. Sarah has built a close relationship with James but also confessed:

> On reflection, perhaps I have been doing too much for James. After observing him today I can see that although initially he found it difficult to fit in, he figured out a way to get involved and play with the others. He does tend to rely on me when we do more structured activities, so from this free play I have learnt that I need to let him do more for himself. That's going to be quite hard for me! (Interview, May 2009)

Further discussion with Sarah revealed that she had been taking the role of Key Person very seriously and had felt both privileged yet anxious to provide the best possible support for James. She had taken 'You must plan for each child's individual care and learning requirements' (DCSF, 2008e: 6) literally and the cardboard box play demonstrated to her that she could allow James to have autonomy, and that while he may not have met his own needs initially, he was ingenious enough to figure out a way to be involved. She reflected:

> I find the EYFS documentation difficult. On the one hand it is very woolly and vague, saying play should underpin everything we do. What does that mean? It has created a lot of stress in our setting – and then it can also be very prescriptive and you think, 'right, well at least I know where I am with that', but then, like I have done with James, you take it too literally and still end up worrying if you are doing the right thing for the child. (Interview, May 2009)

The personal battle Sarah demonstrates here is something that many practitioners experience. The way in which the EYFS is perceived and the way play is interpreted are vitally important. They set the tone for what you do and how you respond to all children's play needs regardless of their background or individual needs. To support children in developing a 'unique self' they must be supported in following their own interests where the motivation for them to engage with other children and different play materials comes from them. It is important that these interests are not imposed by practitioners via outcome-driven activities (however hard this may be for you). Play is initiated by children – to satisfy their own curiosity, to push their own boundaries, to master new skills, to build new relationships, to explore their environment, and for a number of other needs, some of which will not always be clear to practitioners. However, in providing the space where children will be able to follow their own play interests you are building children's foundations for them to express who they are in relation to the world. Katz (1993) has suggested that while this appears to be intangible, it does in fact value the process of unpacking what children do when they engage in self-directed play opportunities. The challenge for the practitioner is to recognise that this play must be owned by the child and not by the adult. For quality play to emerge it must be child initiated and led, with practitioners only taking a role when invited to by the child.

Continuing Professional Development Activity

It is important to have a shared understanding of what play means in your setting. One way of moving towards an answer is to agree what is *not* play. This is necessary because when you find something difficult to articulate it is often easier to define what it is not rather than what it is. However, this is only a starting point. The process of reaching a consensus on how you approach play can be quite arduous: there is no 'quick fix' if you want this to be effective and to help new and existing members of staff to really understand what it means for play to underpin practice.

The Mosaic Approach with your team – what is play?

Aim

- To support your practice in thinking about what play means to you.

- To share your ideas of play in a visual and oral format.

- To stimulate discussion and pull together key themes which may help in forming your setting's definition of play.

 ### Activity

This activity requires you to take photos in your setting of those examples that you believe represent play. These photos should remain exclusively for this activity and should follow your settings policy for taking photographs and gaining consent. If you are unable to take photographs you can adapt the activity to describing play rather than visually representing it.

1 Gather together enough digital or disposable cameras for your team.

2 Think about what play means to you and allow 30–60 minutes (depending on the number of colleagues and size of the setting) to take pictures of anything in that setting that significantly represents play to you. At the end of this activity you will need to explain why you have chosen to take pictures of particular things, so ensure your pictures have a purpose and are not random shots of the environment.

3 You will need to download or process the pictures and print them for the second half of the activity.

4 Devise some ground rules for the following discussion. These might include: being respectful of other people's views; allowing everyone to contribute; keeping the discussion focused on 'what is play?'; listening to each other and minimising diversions into other issues.

5   Spread the pictures out on a table and start a discussion by looking for the similarities in the pictures that you and your colleagues have taken.

6   Any discussion should focus on the diverse set of pictures you will be presented with. Facilitate this discussion away from individual photographs and try to draw out the common themes. This may include the outside environment, specific toys/games, or a particular space within the setting.

7   The discussion will feature different views, such as what you consider a stimulating play space to be. It is important to explore these various outlooks further and to understand other people's perspectives without this becoming personal. If that does start to happen, try to refocus on the aims of the activity.

8   Set a date for a review of the activity. This needs to be about 7–10 days after the event. In the meantime, set up a message book or use a whiteboard to write down the common themes and perhaps a definition of your setting's ideals for play. In the review/reflection period you and your colleagues will then be able to add to or change the statements made by others.

9   At the review of the activity focus on what children are experiencing when they play, what they are learning, saying, exploring and discovering. What impact has it had on how you view play? What made you record or take the photographs you did?

Questions to consider

• *How challenging did you find this activity?*

Some people are able to complete this activity very quickly if they have a definite view of what play is. Others will take longer in selecting what they want to photograph. It is important that the activity is taken seriously and valued, otherwise you will just end up with a series of meaningless pictures. Some people may become frustrated during the activity as they may not be able to find what they think play is. This is quite rare, but if it does happen encourage staff to reflect on why they cannot find what they are looking for and then open this up for discussion when you have the pictures in front of everyone.

• *What have you learned from the experience?*

The activity helps staff to re-evaluate what they think play is and how they can provide and resource it in their setting. By taking the photographs it may remind them of their own play experiences or what they have provided for their own children. It is important to focus this question in a professional capacity so the discussion does not become centred on a trip down memory lane. It has to have relevance to your practice and provide a basis for further discussion. You may choose to highlight common themes or any strategies you use to support play, or you might want to use your reflection to start to make changes to your practice.

- *What will you do with the information that you have gathered from the activity?*

As a team you will need to decide what you will do with the material you have collected. Part of the aim is to reflect on a personal understanding of play, but more significantly to work towards a definition of play for your setting. This does not have to be set in stone at the end of the activity and can be developed over a period of time. If you have a white board or message book in your staff room it is worthwhile to try to write down what you have achieved from the activity, how your feelings towards play have changed or developed, or perhaps to have a go at writing a setting definition. This can then be available for everyone to view over the following weeks and then to discuss this period of reflection at your next team meeting.

Summary

Not only is the child central to the process of play, but also the way in which you respond to children's actions and reactions within play is crucial to the success of children in developing their unique qualities. The more opportunities there are that can provide the potential to direct their own outcomes, to practise their skills and explore their own autonomy, the more children will develop a sense of who they are. It is important that throughout this process practitioners consider the impact of how they interpret and apply the principles of the EYFS on children's play experiences. Consequently, as a team, it is important to know what 'play-based practice' means to your setting and how you interpret the EYFS documentation.

2

Celebrating Children's Play Choices

Natalie Canning

Chapter Objectives

In this chapter key themes emerge in supporting children to engage with free play opportunities and to express their unique qualities. Certain factors must be in place to enable this to happen, such as trusting children and recognising the power relationships adults and practitioners hold over children's play. Considering adult participation and the way in which their values and beliefs can influence play is also explored. Listening to the child's voice through their play choices is examined and linked to the subjective nature of observations and the implications this has for future play opportunities.

Trusting play

The previous chapter considered the idea of children choosing their play freely as a basis for it to occur spontaneously. It is important to explore this in more detail in order to identify the different facets of play, how these are central to children's development, and how our understanding of play affects what we do in practice. The EYFS states that 'every area of development – physical, cognitive, linguistic, spiritual, social and emotional is equally important' to children's development (DCSF, 2008a: 1) and play is one of the ways in which these areas of development can be underpinned. It should be central to the holistic experience offered to children through not seeing it as something separate to everything else that children do, but as part of the way in which children engage with the world. Equally, children's development should not be compartmentalised into different areas although it is easier to organise our thinking and planning in this way as it fits with the systems (Ofsted, for example) and subsequent parental expectations of practice. Practitioners do feel pressured to deliver outcomes and produce paperwork which ultimately impacts on the time available to spend with children.

Children do not organise themselves into different areas of development and therefore it is important to see play, learning and development emerging on a continuum, recognising the skills, qualities and competencies a child has within a given play situation, celebrating their choices, and recognising how to develop their interests further (Broadhead, 2006). In moving towards a more holistic approach to play practitioners also move closer to understanding how it can underpin practice. However, in order to do this the gap that exists between the rhetoric of believing freely chosen play should be available for children and the reality of this within early years settings needs to be reduced. When questioned, practitioners will nearly always respond in the same way as Cherry, the preschool manager in the case study:

> I have a degree in Early Years, I know the importance of a play-based curriculum and I know it is important to offer free choice to children in my setting. It sounds simple, but I have found it really difficult to implement. I think this is because my default is to make sure everything is planned and organised, just in case Ofsted walks through the door. I guess it comes down to not trusting my knowledge of the children to justify free play to them [Ofsted]. (Interview, May 2009)

Cherry reveals here a common anxiety for early years practitioners. She believes in the benefits of free play opportunities but does not quite trust herself to take the risk of providing children with such opportunities on a regular basis in her setting. Guilbaud (2003) argues that the essence of play is when children are trusted to make their own decisions, to test out new ideas, and to enter their own play world. Practitioners should be prepared to enable this to happen, but it does rely on a balance of trust and respect in the relationships existing between practitioners and children. It is important that these qualities are developed by:

• recognising each child as an individual;

• knowing the children well enough to acknowledge their individual knowledge, skills, competencies and their understanding of their world;

- knowing their strengths and the challenges they face, not only in the setting but also at home and in their wider community;

- building a sense of trust by giving them responsibility;

- promoting a sense of ownership in terms of the resources, layout and decoration of the setting;

- supporting children to feel that they belong and are valued for who they are.

Before the cardboard box play in the case study, Cherry reflected on the fact that she was nervous of what would happen and how the children would react. She felt it was a risk because it was something different that *she* had never tried before. She was worried about:

- how the children would interact;

- whether the children with additional needs would be included if support from key workers was not provided;

- whether the children would accept and play with those children that they wouldn't normally socialise with;

- how the children would react to being rejected by other children.

Generally the preschool practitioners would facilitate these issues between children to ensure any conflict was dealt with using a nurturing capacity. Because of this approach the children in the cardboard box play were able to transpose the same principles into their free play; for example, in the case study James was invited by William to join in with the fireman game. It is essential that children are exposed to diverse experiences in early childhood to support their development. Bandura (1962) argued that it was important that children build a sense of self-efficacy where via different experiences they could build a self-belief about their effectiveness and competence. Developing these attitudes enables children to cope with particular situations. The play interactions that children encounter help them to practise and develop their understanding of the patterns that make up social relationships and friendship. In free play it is particularly revealing to observe the choices children make in terms of their engagement depending on how self-assured they feel to actively participate. This is because when children make play choices they can use opportunities to make decisions about their engagement and behaviour. They can be innovative in their thinking and apply this to their play situation to develop strategies that will be accepted into the play (Smith, 2010). For example, in the case study James was aware that William had seen him being rejected by Peter and therefore stood a chance of being accepted into his game. In a one-to-one session after the play, William confirmed that he had felt sorry for James and that was why he invited him to play with him. Erikson (1963) has also recognised that in play children are able to be autonomous in a way they cannot be anywhere else. This was true for James, who demonstrated his self-assurance and a level of autonomy to show that he wanted to be a part of the play and persisted in this until he was accepted into the game.

The preschool team reflected at the end of the session that they needed to trust children to create their own play contexts and to allow them to take the lead in negotiating their own play relationships and conflict resolutions. They also recognised that while the children were engaged in play they had an important job to do in carrying out detailed observations, which could provide them with insights for more structured activities to develop some of the skills demonstrated in free play. They reflected that they had become 'stuck' in the experiences they were offering at the preschool, dominated by a routine which restricted the teams' ability to think outside the box. It also highlighted the fact that play started with the child, that they were the experts in their own play, and that they needed to trust the rich experiences they could gain from freely chosen play experiences.

Participation in play

In considering children's unique qualities it is important to recognise how you are able to support children's development. Not all children will flourish in free play situations all of the time. Therefore sensitive practice is required to understand the way children communicate their needs through verbal and non-verbal gestures. Responding and interpreting children's intention at the start or during play is important in allowing reciprocal play relationships to develop between yourself and the children involved. Hughes (1999) emphasises the importance of developing secure relationships with children and suggests that a key element of this lies in accepting children for who they are at a given point in time, recognising their strengths, and knowing when support is required. Identifying these qualities through play situations can enable practitioners to assess covertly where the child is in aspects of development such as emotional, social, cognitive and motor skills. The EYFS states 'you must plan for each child's individual care and learning requirements' (DCSF, 2008e: 6). However, the way in which you do this relies on you having an understanding of the child as an individual and their lived experiences inside and outside of the setting. Having such knowledge of individual circumstances will enable you to 'read' children's play and make judgements about why they choose to play in certain ways. For example, if you know a child is experiencing anxiety at home you may see frustration or anger emerge in that child's play. Equally, children may avoid play situations that make them feel uncomfortable (such as physical play) if they do not feel they have the skills or ability to participate.

This is when a sensitive adult participation in play can support children's emotional wellbeing. In many situations this will happen at an intuitive level when you do not realise you are supporting a child's ability to succeed in a play situation. However, practitioner participation in play can also be deliberate in order to support a child in moving beyond something with which they are having difficulty (Bruner, 1966). This requires a skilled practitioner who can recognise a child's feelings and attempt to reflect them back to that child through mirroring play and supporting them in working through the emotional triggers that the situation evokes. Fisher (2008) identifies that the way in which practitioners engage with children can have an immediate effect on their level of involvement. This in turn can lead to a positive interaction where both child and practitioner are immersed in the play as mutual play partners. In contrast, if the practitioner misinterprets the signals being given by children this can result in them trying to escape the play situation. How often have you observed children trying to move away from a busy play space? This physical movement on the part of the child represents their need to disengage from the adult world and re-establish their play (Canning, 2007). Children may not verbalise how they feel when met with an ill-timed intervention from a practitioner but will demonstrate their discomfort through, for example, self-conscious play behaviour. Therefore, in entering into the child's world of play, it is essential to:

- respect and recognise the child's agenda for their play and follow their lead;

- respond appropriately within the context of the play;

- support a climate of permissiveness where objects can be used as and how the child wants, without enforcing an end outcome;

- respect the play and its significance to the child;

- allow the child to lead you through the play and follow their lead;

- engage in the play until the child has 'played out' their agenda (you may not really know when this has happened, but watch for a change in the play or behaviour of the child);

- provide a sense of security and reassurance.

It is important that you start from a 'can do', positive perspective when facilitating children's play. It is easy to slip into a restrictive attitude of 'I can't let a child do this in case it turns into disruptive play or behaviour', but this returns to the point of firstly knowing the children in your care and trusting them to make positive play choices. It is also about having the confidence and strategies to support children in a positive environment where negative play behaviour can be quickly and effectively managed. This means that as well as a trusting ethos in play, you also need to balance the power relationships between yourself as the adult/practitioner and children's play.

Power in play

We have established that practitioners have a central role when children play. You have control over the play space, planning and organising the resources needed, how they will be set out, the timetable for the day, and how play could develop into new learning opportunities. Practitioners hold power over the play space, shaping children's interests and direction. It is logical then to make the argument that when you make these decisions these are based on:

- having a knowledge of individual children's needs;

- having an understanding of play and child development through undertaking qualifications and CPD sessions;

- practising observation, assessment and planning on a regular basis;

- working with policy documentation on a practical level;

- having the confidence to let go of control and follow the children's lead.

However, Kalliala (2009) argues that when practitioners start to take this process for granted and work in well-established routines they begin to become complacent and lose sight of providing opportunities for children to express their individuality and also for opportunities to closely observe children. In a normal working day observations of children are limited to 'snapshots' of what they are doing, usually recorded hastily to be written up in more detail at a later date. It is rare for practitioners to have the opportunity to really observe the processes that children are involved in and to reflect on what this means for the individual child. Burke (2008) discusses how the space that children and practitioners occupy can have a disproportionate aspect of power, in terms of culture and what is expected in relation to behaviour and rules, and how this can limit children in their exploration of physical space and imaginative capacity. She states that settings can 'set out their own rhythms of time that children learn early and unless they resist, cleave to' (Burke, 2008: 27). The imbalance of power tipped towards the practitioner is something that usually goes unnoticed. The 'adult world' will almost always trump the 'child's world': how often have you witnessed or said the following?

- 'Stop playing now, it's time for a snack' (without negotiating with the child at the beginning of the play session).

- 'I'll come and play with you in a minute; I just need to finish this first.'

- 'You are only allowed to go so high.'

- 'We can't go outside because it is raining.'

- 'Why don't you play with this?'

These are just a few of the statements which while they may be applied for good reasons illustrate how power stays firmly within an adult/practitioner-led capacity, even when attempting to facilitate a child-led environment. Burke (2008: 26) recognises that play is a key element in children's culture and how it is important to understand 'subversive, hidden and intimate aspects of their play'. She argues that research into this area of children's lives is significant, but warns against adults' inclination to want to know about and control all aspects of children's lives. This is supported by Hughes (2001) who claims that adults are hijacking play to ensure their own agenda is fulfilled rather than placing the child at the centre of the process. Freire (1970) balanced these views by highlighting that it was important to recognise the richness of children's play culture but also that this could reveal tensions in unequal relationships of power between children and practitioners in settings. In providing a way to reconcile this tension, Kalliala (2009) advocates for a correlation between the practitioner as an 'activator' of children's interest and the subsequent engagement of the child in play. This means that the practitioner supports an initial intervention to start the play which may lead to rich play opportunities for the children. The case study is an example of how Cherry, the preschool manager, 'activated' the children's play by removing the usual resources and dedicating the space to various cardboard boxes.

Kalliala also recognises that in the role of 'activator' the practitioner needs to be able to balance the power relationship between the adult world and child world by allowing their children autonomy within the play situation. Children who have choice and freedom within their play are empowered to use and develop their own observation skills (Canning, 2007). This is clear in the case study when Shona observes Eva becoming frustrated when her cardboard box tower keeps falling down. It is Shona's choice to enter into Eva's play and Eva's choice to let her do so. This reciprocal play relationship demonstrates an ability by both girls to have autonomy in their individual play choices but also to experience empowerment. Shona is empowered because she has helped Eva achieve something that she was struggling with on her own. She had the confidence to approach Eva and offer her help and to develop her problem-solving skills in putting her idea of forming a base for the tower into practice. Eva is empowered as her aim of building a tower is achieved out of a sense of initial frustration. Children will frequently watch a play situation develop before they attempt to invite themselves into a play space in order to assess how 'safe' they feel and how involved they want to become in the interactions with others (Canning, 2007). In the case study all of the children were given the opportunity to experiment with autonomy as they had freedom within the practitioner-activated play. This then empowered the children to experiment with making decisions based on their assessment of the situation. The children in this section of the case study also demonstrated equality between the players. They worked together to solve a problem regardless of their age, experience, gender and ability. This naturally created a more inclusive play and learning environment.

Seeing and listening to children

Kalliala warns that practitioners must be skilled in knowing when to 'activate' and when to enable children to initiate their own play.

This requires that you not only evaluate the balance within your setting of adult *vs*. child-initiated play but also that you develop your skills in 'seeing' when children need that extra support and knowing when to leave them to figure it out for themselves or with peers. Generally we are anxious to help children find the solution to a problem or assist them in mastering a skill, but it is essential that children are also given time in play to practise these skills on their own. In recognising the balance between child/adult-initiated play in your setting this also requires you to think about your underlying assumptions about the qualities children possess and demonstrate during play. For example, Qvortrup et al. (1994: 2) viewed children as 'beings not becomings'. They bring something of themselves to every situation which enhances their experience and the experience of others. From this viewpoint it is vital that children's voices and their play choices are recognised and heard. These are usually most prominent when they are engaged in play over which they have control. It is not only children's voices that are important but also the way in which they are interpreted and children's behaviours are observed. This returns to the theme of trusting children's ability to be 'experts in their own lives' (Langsted, 1994: 42) and experts in their own play. Mayall (2002) views children's engagement in play as a construction of knowledge, ideas and meanings. It is then the role of the practitioner to find a way to represent the child's voice in terms of celebrating their development and recognising where they need support. The EYFS states:

> Practitioner's observations of children help them to assess the progress which children are making. Observations help practitioners to decide where children are in their learning and development and plan what to do. (DCSF, 2008e: 11)

This statement relies on practitioners making sound judgements and interpretations of what children are engaged in when they play. This is reliant on the knowledge, understanding, values and beliefs of practitioners, but also on the capacity of the setting to recognise how observations can be interpreted and what this means for individual children and their development. To make observations meaningful, they need to do more than just record what is happening, but by making a more subjective/interpretive observation it is important to recognise that other colleagues may have viewed the same play in a different way. For example, during the cardboard box play in the case study, the preschool team undertook observations of their key children. Jodie was observing Peter who was playing by himself. This was one of her observations:

Table 2.1 Jodie's observation – cardboard box play

Child Peter	Date 9th May 2009	Practitioner Jodie	Situation Cardboard box play

What is happening?

Peter is playing alone. He has placed several cardboard boxes around him and is pretending to be in a racing car with an imaginary steering wheel, leaning over as he goes around the corners, making car engine sounds. He is happy to play alone and when James wants to join in he tells him to go away.

Next Steps? 1 PSED 2 Comm, Lang & Lit 3 Prob. Sol, Reason, Numeracy 4 K&UW 5 Physical Dev 6 Creative Dev	• Mix of social and peer play opportunities. • Co-operative play opportunities. • Discussions about others feelings – needs of others. • Use of boxes to support shape, space and measures (interest in boxes). • Extend interest in design and making (cars). • Experiment with different materials to build on imaginative play. • Questions about Peter's play when he has made something or been involved in imaginative play. • Explore different materials following a similar theme of cars. • More opportunities for imaginative play.

The observation tells you what Peter is doing, the functions of his play, but does not offer an interpretation of the processes he is engaged in. This means that the 'planning for next steps' section is concerned with the development of relationships and as Jodie later reflected 'perhaps the next steps part has the wrong focus' (Interview, May 2009). In order to analyse the processes involved in Peter's play Jodie could have made judgements about what Peter was doing, thinking and feeling through her knowledge of Peter's personality, her understanding of the relationship between Peter and James, and her knowledge of child development. This more subjective account would have provided a different interpretation in planning for future play opportunities. For example, she could have highlighted that Peter was:

• showing a preference in who he wanted to play with;

• making decisions about the direction of his play;

• being self-confident in saying 'no' to James's request to join in the play;

• showing independence;

• demonstrating high levels of involvement;

• expressing his feelings in an appropriate way;

- expressing own voice and play needs;

- demonstrating high levels of imaginative and creative play.

There is no 'right' or 'wrong' answer in analysing the approach to these examples of observation, but what it does highlight is the scope of interpretation and the way in which the practitioner can influence the observation, even if they are not an active part of the play, just by the way in which they record what they 'see'. The preschool team reflected that they often concerned themselves with the functions of play. In reviewing the children's personal learning journey diaries – a notebook containing pictures, comments and observations of the children's time at the preschool – they reflected that there was very little analysis about how the children reached goals and outcomes just that they had been able to achieve them. The outcomes superseded the quality of the children's play and the 'voice' that they were demonstrating through their play choices. Jodie reflected that another way to analyse the observations would be to ask the children what they thought about the play after they had finished. This would provide her with the child's perspective and a potential insight into a personal experience of play.

Continuing Professional Development Activity

Jackson (2010: 176) asks 'How is quality measured?' and responds by looking at how government uses minimum measurable welfare requirements for state registration and the inspection of early year settings. These form part of the EYFS curriculum learning and development requirements, assuring parents that 'essential standards of provision are in place' (DCSF, 2008f: 10) no matter which type of setting they access for their child. The 'top down' measures of the Children Act 2006, Office for Standards in Education (Ofsted), Every Child Matters (DfES, 2004), *Raising Standards – Improving Outcomes* (DCSF, DoH, DWP, 2006) and the National Quality Improvement Network (NQIN, 2007) ensure that these minimum quality assurances are in place – however, how does this translate to a 'bottom up' approach in practice? The following activity may provide your setting with a starting point for discussion.

Where are the choices and voices in play?

Aim

- To consider what quality play looks like in your setting from a 'bottom up' approach.

- To share perspectives on how you facilitate hearing and seeing a child's play world through a balance of trust, power and participation.

 Activity

Before you start this activity it may be useful to have a discussion about the themes raised in this chapter. Some of the questions and resulting answers may raise other issues about quality and conflicting perspectives. It is important that whoever facilitates this activity is sensitive to every team member's experience and opinion.

1 Ask each member of staff to draw four scales on one piece of paper from 0%–100%.

0 ————————————— 50% —————————————100%

2 Label each scale:

- Autonomy.

- Participation.

- Power.

- Choice.

3 Then ask colleagues to think about their own practice and honestly score themselves under each of the headings while asking the following questions (reassure them first that all answers will remain anonymous):

- What level of autonomy do you give to children when they play?

- How often do you participate in children's play (invited or uninvited)?

- How much do you think you influence children's play choices (power question)?

- What percentage of play do you provide that is based on children's free choice?

4 Collect the results and repeat the activity using the same scale, but this time ask colleagues to consider the setting as a whole and not just their individual practice, for example:

- How much autonomy do children have in their play?

- What level of adult participation is there in children's play?

- How much power does the setting have in children's play choices?

- What percentage of play involves children's free choice?

It will help you to analyse the results as a team if the personal perspective and setting perspective is completed in different colours to aid comparisons.

5 Collect the results and use them as a basis for a discussion on the differences and similarities between personal and setting perspectives. It will help if you cut the completed scales up so you are able to compare them under the headings (this also aids anonymity for individuals).

6 From this activity consider if, as a team, you hold the same picture of 'quality' for the setting and if not why this might be so.

7 Consider how you might adapt this kind of activity to ask the children in your setting about their experiences of play. This may deliver some surprising results and support your development in terms of what you think you are delivering in relation to play and what the reality is for the children.

Questions to consider

- *How will you enable the team to express their opinion ensuring anonymity?*

It may be that you position a box where team members can 'post' their completed scales over a set time period in order to be sensitive to anonymity issues. You could also spread this activity over a few weeks so you do not deal with all of the themes at the same time, although they are inter-related and commonalities should emerge from your discussions.

- *What will you do with the information you have gathered from the activity?*

It is important that this activity is not seen as something to be done and then forgotten. The issues of listening to children, quality play provision and facilitating play choices are big subject areas, so if you do not find a consensus then don't feel as if the activity has been worthless: the importance of sharing in the discussion and hearing each other's views is equally, if not more, important. There is also a danger that individuals will become self-conscious or possessive about their opinion/ perspective. Try to foster an inclusive environment where all views are valid and redirect conflicting views into how diversity can be facilitated within your setting.

Summary

This chapter has discussed some of the issues surrounding trusting children, power relationships, adult participation in play and listening to children's voices. It has focused on the role and influence of the practitioner in children's play and the significance of this in relation to interpreting the EYFS. Through your practice you will have experienced the many ways in which play can be interpreted, but an emerging theme here is to consider your values and beliefs about quality experiences of free play opportunities for each child to express their unique self. In this chapter the importance of the way in which observations are analysed has been touched upon and this will be developed as you move through the different sections of the book. A single observation has been analysed in two different ways, highlighting the central role practitioners occupy in supporting children's play and the influence they can have on future play opportunities, based on a knowledge and understanding of the child, values and beliefs, and a subjective interpretation of the significance of play.

3

Including and Enabling All Children as Individuals

Mandy Andrews

Chapter Objectives

This chapter outlines current theory relating to children's development within a socio-cultural context and considers how children enter play environments with specific experiences and requirements. It advocates a way of supporting all children's needs and experiences so they become embedded in everyday practice. It demonstrates how practitioners can develop their own practice to extend play opportunities where children's unique qualities, their personal intent, and involvement in play are at the centre of practice.

Play in a cultural context

Research (cited by Smith et al., 2003) has identified that all children can play but that there are socially constructed barriers and drivers which can either enable, extend or restrict access to social play opportunities for children. Everyone has a 'cultural background', originating from family, the local community, country of birth, or place of upbringing. Everyone has a social template embedded from early memories which not only shapes our uniqueness, but also enables us to operate within our communities and familiar routines and rituals. Many parents will recognise how an older child may go to stay with a friend's family and come back with tales of how things are different in their home. As practitioners, recognising difference and appreciating the value of different perspectives on life can help to support the accessibility of play opportunities for all children. Therefore, the definition of 'cultural background' used in this chapter does not merely refer to nationality at birth, and the social context related to that nationality, but also relates to the way that groups of people operate with a shared understanding. These groups of people could be families, communities or the wider religious, ideological, political and social contexts which affect children's play. Similarly, the term 'inclusion' will refer to enabling differentiation and diversity and working positively so that no children are barred or discouraged by either an attitude or environment from actively participating in the play experiences offered.

Rogoff (2003: 368) studied the cultural nature of human development in a range of communities and concluded that 'humans develop through their changing participation in the socio-cultural activities of their communities, which also change'. She understood that not only were children alert to learning from the cultural opportunities and reactions of others around them, but also that children's relationships with other children and adults shape their future experiences and allow for a further interpretation of their social context. For example, the children in the case study may have been motivated to play 'pirates' because of a recent 'cultural' experience of an European fairytale and so were led by this to play 'captain of the ship' games. Another child may have had a very different experience, such as seeing or hearing about a fire drill practice. They perhaps reenacted the sight of the firemen and women and so used their play to make further sense of what they had seen. In the case study some children put the cardboard boxes on their heads and ran around making the 'ne-nar' sound of a siren. It could be argued that cultural experiences were shaping their play. These cultural experiences can be both actual experiences that have been seen and heard, and those emphasised through pictures, story books, or tales told by friends.

Lived experiences

Rogoff (2003) takes this issue further and suggests that the most difficult processes to examine are those that are based on confident and unquestioned assumptions arising from our own common practices. For example, here we could consider television which is often taken for granted in social conversations. There are families who have consciously decided not to have a television in their house in an attempt

to rebalance family life and encourage reading rather than more pas-
sive 'watching'. Yet families in the UK without a television are
relatively rare. For a child growing up in such a family introducing
an activity that is based around a TV series would be difficult for
them to follow. Each child is a product of their changing interactions
with others and aspects of their daily lives which they know, see, or
experience in social contexts. Bronfenbrenner (1979) developed a
model which he termed an 'ecological perspective' to illustrate how
the child is influenced by changing levels of interaction within a
series of rings of influence, from a close family community through
to a very much wider political and social emphasis. The first of these
areas of influence on the child is the immediate family, the
'microsystem' of influence (Bronfenbrenner, 1979). The second refers
to the complex interaction between the child's home and early year's
setting, or the child's local neighbourhood experience. The external
ring relates to the political and broad cultural or ideological environment that influences the child. It is important to recognise the
way in which a child develops and makes transitions from one ring
of influence to the next. During such a transition there will be an element of dialogue between participants, there may be tensions and
areas the child needs to explore, and each existing 'cultural understanding' will be amended as the new circle of influence affects the
direction of the child's development and play.

A child's understanding of how adults behave has to be adjusted when
they are presented with a new set of adults (and related rules and expectations) on entry to an early years setting, a new play room, or indeed
school. Similarly, the expectations of an early year's setting will
inevitably influence a parent's interaction with their children, and parents working in partnership with the setting will also influence the
setting's interaction with children. These are fluid relationships, often
based on 'cultural' issues. The children playing with cardboard boxes in
the case study may have been influenced by their home experiences,
things they had seen in their close neighbourhood, or the experiences
and culture of practitioners who may have influenced them to play in
a certain way. The outer 'spheres' of influence presented in Bronfenbrenner's ecological model are those broader cultural understandings
such as politics, work, education, ideology and the like that impact on
the child beyond their home and immediate setting. This area of influence can include a parent's workplace, which the child may experience
directly (by visiting) or indirectly (through conversation or reports from
others).

Indirect cultural experiences of parent's work may impact on the way
a family operates. Shift working is an example which will impact on

the pattern of family life and its culture. A child with a parent who works night shifts may lay a great emphasis on the need for sleep during the day. Another child may have experience of parents or neighbours working long hours in a corner shop and the activities that relate to running a business of that kind. The child may understand well the particular reasons for their pattern of life, but may equally not understand another child's experience at this point. Their play may then reflect their own experiences (perhaps going into a box and shutting themselves in 'to catch up on sleep' or stacking the cardboard boxes as if on shop shelves). Drawing on observations of life around them, children's play culture inevitably provides an element of 'templating' (providing patterns of social understanding) for a child to work out, compare and practise through play. It is for this reason that children should also be exposed to a range of images and stories, pictures, music and other play resources that can reflect the diversity around them or that they may meet in the future.

The social institutions, the politics, the ideology and pervading culture of the broadest community in which the child exists will also influence their national identity in play. This area of influence recognises that language and customs are different in varying regions of the world. Whilst shops, streets and offices may be very much in operation in many countries, they may look and operate differently if compared between these countries. Children who have visited other countries may 'practise' in their play some of the differences in 'ways of behaving' that they have experienced. Perhaps here the cardboard box becomes the Eiffel tower, or a vast mountain range, they may perhaps become colourful markets or represent a particular experience a child may have had. These may be very stereotyped snapshots of other cultures, but are still valid experiences for the child to explore further in play.

Bronfenbrenner (1979) argues that time should be taken to consider the impact of the different ecological contexts on each child and the influence of the interactions between each of these levels. To do this, practitioners should carefully observe children at play and take time to consider their understandings and motivations. Open-ended play opportunities such as cardboard boxes allow children to demonstrate their social and cultural experiences, rather than being led by the practitioner in culturally biased or culturally neutral activities. Rogoff (2003: 368) argues that 'culture is not just something other people do, but is about understanding our own cultural heritage, perspectives and beliefs, as well as being open to a consideration of the needs of people with contrasting backgrounds'.

Practitioners should be aware that there are different ways of viewing the ideological context (adopted through politics and other perspectives). Ask yourself whether you believe in cultural diversity. Then consider whether you are concerned that certain traditions are being lost in your cultural community. Your resulting views will sit somewhere along a spectrum which ranges from a core belief in the exclusion of other cultures in order to preserve the dominant one at one end of the spectrum, to a celebration of diversity (and difference) at the other. In the middle of this spectrum are varying perspectives in which different cultures are 'assimilated' into a new dominant culture. In an assimilation approach practitioners may respect some aspects of the culture, such as 'food', and discard other aspects which are expected to be adapted to the dominant view – thus, for example, Indian curries become part of the dominant culture's way of life in Western Europe, but the wearing of saris does not. Communities become westernised via dress and the western culture adopts some aspects of Indian culture and so a new assimilated existence is established. It could be argued that assimilation does perhaps dilute cultures, but true diversity celebrates difference at all levels, yet with the inevitable loss of comforting 'sameness'.

Exploring difference in the EYFS

It is important to understand why it is not acceptable to exclude any child on cultural grounds. The EYFS informs us of the need to *'ensure that every child is included and not disadvantaged* because of ethnicity, culture or religion, home language, family background, learning difficulties or disabilities, gender or ability' (DCSF, 2008f: 7) (my emphasis). However, the EYFS goes beyond a basic recognition that there are other cultures and that all children should be included to promote diversity. Booth et al. (2006) argue that for early years practitioners inclusion refers to participation by practitioners as well as an involvement by children in their cultural activities. They state inclusion is about making choices and having a say in practice, but more deeply it is also about being recognised, accepted and valued for ourselves, whether as children or practitioners. This understanding is also evident in the statutory framework for the EYFS in which it states that children should be encouraged to 'have a developing respect for their own cultures and beliefs and those of other people' and also to 'understand that people have different needs, views, cultures and beliefs, that need to be treated with respect' (DCSF, 2008f: 12).

In the case study the cardboard box play does allow children to explore and respect cultural experiences because of its neutrality and flexibility.

It can be adapted to respond to (and so reveal) cultural experiences. However, play is also about children's rights. For a child to adopt self-directed behaviour they must respect their own ability and understanding. Here practitioners' responses of positive affirmation and support are essential. This is the nature of the positive interaction with inclusion that Booth et al. (2006) are referring to. The EYFS does indeed recognise the need to work with diverse experiences while also giving practitioners the potential to adapt the curriculum focus:

> Practitioners should value diversity and provide opportunities for children to develop and use their home language in their play and learning. This is part of respect for each child's cultural background that is central in all early years provision. Alongside support in the home language practitioners should provide a range of meaningful contexts in which children have opportunities to develop English. (DCSF, 2008f: 37)

'Meaningful contexts' are those which build on the child's current understanding and interests. Ideally practitioners would observe children at play, see that there is a recent experience of, for example, a wedding or festival experience that children are trying to explore, and respond by swiftly providing further materials that can be used in play to explore these experiences. Children learn from their experiences, but the opportunity to practise those experiences depends on the availability of appropriate materials, support and environments. Children are able to adapt many materials to symbolise something else, but would still need items of different sizes and dimensions, containers, building materials, fabrics and so on.

Cherry, the preschool manager in the case study, is a reflective inclusive practitioner who is sufficiently aware of her own views and understanding to ensure that her setting is flexible enough to respond to the play 'cues' presented by children (Else and Sturrock, 2000). She ensures that there are positive opportunities for exploration through different and flexible materials and staff encouragement. Rogoff (2003: 299) argues that 'children's play builds on what they observe, but what they have the opportunity to observe differs greatly'. Play is an opportunity to gain new experiences, combined with an intrinsic motivation and the provision of appropriate resources that can enable a child to participate in socio-cultural exploration with 'intent'. To support children's cultural play with intent a practitioner must both provide opportunities for these experiences and support the exploration of relevant contexts through usable resources. Rogoff notes that this happens all over the world and so very young children are seen undertaking quite complex tasks relevant to their home or cultural environment as they have been given encouragement and the materials to practise these.

Perspectives of inclusion – the medical model of disability

The EYFS clearly indicates that a key principle is recognising the 'unique' child – whereby 'every child is a competent learner from birth who can be resilient, capable, confident and self-assured' (DCSF, 2008f: 9). Each child is capable, but unique, and therefore, in comparison with another, perhaps also has specific needs. These needs may be just as much those of gifted and talented children as children with a development delay or physical impairment. However, I have often heard practitioners say to each other 'That's my SEN child', thereby highlighting the different need before using the child's name. So often it is the developmental delay that practitioners look for in their assessments, identifying a failure to meet targets as difference and seeking to work to improve that development. This approach – of identifying a possible deficit in a child and working with a focus on improving the child's development chances through targeting or specialised support – is the *medical model* (Brisenden, 2000) approach to disability. This model assumes that there is a concept of a 'normal child' against whom all other children can be measured. If other children cannot meet that 'normal' model (perhaps as a result of sensory impairment, or limited mobility or understanding) then the assumption is that steps should be taken to ensure that children are supported to attain as close to the 'norm' as possible. They may be seen as having a deficit and given hearing aids, wheelchairs, prosthetic limbs and carefully scripted behavioural templates to ensure that they can function as 'normally' as possible. However, there is another way of looking at the way this intervention can take place.

All children have strengths and using practice can work to those strengths rather than be prompted by a deficit approach. In the case study James had a speech delay but this did not restrict him from participating in the play. So often there will be different areas of strength in children who display limitations in one aspect of development. As practitioners it is important to put aside our expectations and to see what children with difficulties affecting one area of development *can* do rather than focusing on what they *cannot* do. In allowing the opportunity for them to explore their strengths and abilities and demonstrate new skills this approach rejects a normative pattern, in which assumptions will sometimes restrict the opportunity for development. Play opportunities, being intrinsically motivated, are usually something a child wants to do, providing experiences through which they may challenge themselves. Play actively challenges boundaries and limitations (Hughes, 2001).

I was recently involved in a play activity at a festival that included an inflatable assault course. A young girl came up to me and asked 'Is it ok if my friend has a go?' I said 'Of course' and then looked at her friend who I then noticed clearly had a visual impairment. She was being led around the festival by her friend, clearly enjoying herself, but with much use of her hands to feel her way. I admit that I had a moment of doubt when I realised the extent of her visual limitations. The assault course was bouncy, it had a two metre vertical rope net climb and a steep slide at the end, not to mention various other obstacles along the way. But on the positive side, she had a friend to support her, I only allowed two children go through at any time, and there were staff there to 'catch' children all the way round. She was thus able to have a go and in so doing I had challenged my own prejudice. Given the chance to be adventurous this young girl not only made her way through the assault course without a great deal of assistance from her friend or the staff, doing much of the work by touch, but also apparently managed to memorise the route and then return many times that afternoon, without any assistance, and to 'race' other children. Her strength lay in her other heightened skills and her amazing memory. I certainly learnt a swift lesson. It would have been so easy to have said 'No, it is too risky, I don't think this is for you' at the beginning, thus curtailing her ability to extend her experiences socially, cognitively and physically there and then.

This experience taught me a valuable lesson about my own prejudices. It reminded me that all practitioners should reflect on their own reactions to opportunities for inclusion. It is a legal duty to ensure that all children with a disability, including those with learning difficulties, will be supported in early years settings. Practitioners are also required to consider how 'reasonable adjustments' will be made for children (DCSF, 2008f: 25). Indeed, all settings and all local authorities (in England) are covered by the Disability Discrimination Act, 2005 (DDA). The definition of disability includes people who have 'a physical or mental impairment which has a substantial and long-term adverse effect on a person's ability to perform normal day-to-day activities' (OPSI, 2005). This encompasses a wide range of impairments, including those that may be hidden. If, for example, a child has an impairment affecting their mobility, sight or hearing, or has learning difficulties, a mental health condition, epilepsy, autism, a speech, language or communication impairment, asthma or diabetes, then he or she may have a disability if the effect of the impairment on their ability to carry out 'normal' day-to-day activities is 'substantial' and 'long-term'. These different elements in the definition mean that, in practice, a much larger group of children will meet the definition of disability than most practitioners would realise (DfES, 2005a). In addition practitioners should be aware that many disabled children will also have special educational needs (SEN) as defined in the Education Act 1996 (OPSI, 1996). All settings and all local education authorities (LEAs) also have duties under the SEN legislation to make provision to meet special educational needs. These duties align with the DDA duties which focus on a protection from discrimination and the removal of barriers through pre-emptive action.

So what does a practitioner have to do to ensure all children are enabled and included? In the case study allowing all the children to participate supported a situation where the play was inclusive of children with a range of abilities and levels of development. Michael did display challenging behaviour generally in the setting, but in the case study he was ignored by the other children when he demanded to be the captain. Nonetheless, he continued to enjoy and gain benefit from the play. The other children had gained a social understanding of how to deal with his challenging behaviour as exemplified by their taking over his 'den'. He continued to be involved in the play and social interaction carried on appropriately without a need for adult intervention. The play offered the potential for him to pursue his needs in his own way and to continue to develop his social skills in context.

Such inclusion through child-led 'play' is not unusual. Smith et al. (2003) cites research which indicates that play which is not adult led leads to increased social interaction and less aggression in children in classroom situations. Hughes (2001: 259) argues that 'play is a very complex phenomenon, but one that stimulates flexibility in the child who is playing'. He provides evidence from a range of sources that play opportunities can support children with skills to form novel solutions to problems and that 'the more a child plays in an experientially enriched place the better he or she will be at solving those problems and performing those complex tasks essential for survival and development'. Children know best what they can do and will generally explore these opportunities. By providing play spaces with flexible resources like cardboard boxes practitioners are allowing any children with impairments to seek novel solutions that are appropriate to them at the time. The girl at the festival found a solution by aligning with her (perhaps braver) friend who opened the door for her experiences by effectively 'asking questions' of me as a practitioner.

Perspectives of inclusion – the social model of disability

In the case study the active removal of barriers to access the materials was more akin to the *social model* of disability (Barnes,

2000). In the social model it is recognised that it is not the person with the impairment who is responsible for their disabled situation, but a society that creates restrictions and prevents individuals from being active participants in their own way. Expectations embedded in the culture of our society effectively 'disable' individuals with specific needs. An example here was my attitude (had it been followed through) that the assault course was 'too risky' for the young girl at the festival. I could have easily set up a barrier to her development and sense of achievement, based on my own perceptions and concerns. Research for the DfES on ways to improve access for the early years (DfES, 2005a) identified that most practitioners' understanding of promoting inclusion was generally limited to a few examples and that one of the main development areas for staff was to gain greater understanding of the range and number of children who require support. This does not mean that all practitioners should have a complete awareness of every aspect of what constitutes a special need. The statutory guidance to the EYFS does not require this, but it does require an awareness of attitude, adequate space, and the ease of access to any specialist resources required.

A positive attitude to inclusion can allow all children to play – and play in turn allows for increased social skills, supports a greater understanding of ability, and consequently promotes positive attitudes in others. However, it is important not to assume there is some utopian vision in which all practitioners will have positive attitudes, enabling every child to play equally and flourish at their own level. Chappell (2000) argues that the social model groups all people together. She indicates that striking a balance to a more individualist approach is part of the journey towards a modern interpretation of inclusion in which situations are accessible to all, but within which individual voices can be heard. Practitioners need to be aware that having an impairment (or a different cultural experience) in common with another child does not necessarily mean that they have other things in common. It is important that we do not assume that a child fits into some sort of general pattern for that particular impairment or experience, nor should we assume that we will be able to easily identify a child's specific need. It is therefore important to carefully observe, promote and learn from children themselves and their parents or carers. If a flexible approach is taken in response to the child's needs and experiences, by a practitioner who recognises their own potential prejudicial images and reactions, then all children can be included regardless of their disability, culture or gender.

Continuing Professional Development Activity

So far we have considered different aspects of supporting children as individuals through inclusion, celebrating difference, focusing on attitudes and perceptions and highlighting challenges for children to explore their unique qualities. The child remains at the centre of this process, yet the practitioner has a pivotal role in providing play opportunities that can support participation and inclusion through open-ended resources.

Table 3.1 Range of resources for open-ended play

Potential open-ended resources	Key questions and reflection
1. Example: Cardboard boxes	How will the resource be used? Consider: • The space available. • The level of challenge presented by the resource. • The way that children might be encouraged to design and use the space and/or resource as they wish. How might you promote a recognition of cultural diversity through this resource? What limitations in terms of access, resources, staffing or time might there be? How could these be overcome?

Identifying the potential in open-ended resources

Aims

• To identify open-ended resources that can motivate and stimulate play opportunities.

• To explore and reflect on your practice in providing inclusive opportunities for children.

 Activity

1 Use the table above to consider a range of resources that could be provided for open-ended play that would be appropriate for all children to participate in.

2 An example using cardboard boxes as in the case study has been suggested as your first open-ended resource.

3 Consider the questions in the second column and reflect on what you would do with your resources and how the resulting play could be inclusive and encourage participation.

4 You should discuss the questions with colleagues from your setting to share different perspectives and highlight any disparity in your approaches to resources and inclusion. Try to be honest about your own practice and identify through a discussion with colleagues how your thinking may have changed in light of this chapter.

5 You can add as many potential open-ended resources as you can think of to the table. Use the activity not only to celebrate good practice, but also to encourage creative ideas that you could implement in your setting in the future.

Question to consider

• *How will you continue to enable all children to celebrate their unique qualities?*

Ensuring that your setting is inclusive and meets all children's needs is challenging. It requires an ability to know the individual needs of each child in your care and support them in developing their personality, skills and learning. You will be able to identify the ways in which you can meet these needs and hopefully this chapter has provided you with some new perspectives and ideas for developing your practice. The key theme of this chapter is that the child is at the centre of the process. By providing opportunities through play to support children's development, you are contributing to the exploration of their unique qualities and building confidence and experiences of new situations and interactions. Although this may be challenging it is important to provide resources that can be flexible and accessible. In this way you are developing your practice in order to help children understand and experience equality, difference and diversity.

Summary

This chapter has introduced the importance of seeing each child within a socio-cultural context and explored the social and medical models of inclusion and approaches to practice. It has considered issues about inclusive practice and play, with the important theme that child-led play can support inclusion and participation where children are able to negotiate within the play space to meet their own needs. Practitioners' attitudes towards inclusion in relation to facilitating play through flexible resources have also been explored. The central message here has been a need to view inclusion as requiring the time to appreciate differences and tailor support so that all children can participate and celebrate their unique qualities.

Section 2

Positive Relationships

'Positive relationships describe how children learn to be strong and independent from a base of loving and secure relationships with parents and/or a key person. The commitments are focused around respect, partnership with parents, supporting learning and the role of the key person.' (DCSF, 2008f: 9)

Positive Relationships

 Case Study: Play and Family Support in a Children's Centre

Rosie Walker

This case study is based on a longitudinal study of one family who has received support from a Children's Centre. The study focusses upon the mother and her three children who are under the age of two years old.

Josie lives in a flat with her partner on the second storey of a council block in a neighbourhood with few leisure or community facilities. Josie is twenty and became involved with the Children's Centre when her first child, Josh, was six months old. She first attended a parental support group called the Bumps and Babes Group on the recommendation of her health visitor, who also brought her to the sessions. Josie was nervous and lacked confidence in managing Josh. She was encouraged to find ways to play and learn with Josh and to understand how her positive and caring influence would help him to understand the world around him.

One of the sessions that Josie and Josh really enjoyed was the treasure basket and heuristic play. Josie recognised that she could provide play opportunities at home by using everyday objects or things she could collect from the park such as pine cones. She was amazed by the way in which Josh could make his preferences known at such a young age by choosing from a range of materials. He especially liked the wooden spoons and soon found out that if he banged it on an upturned sweet tin he could get his mother's attention.

These sessions also provided an opportunity for Josie to meet other parents and to borrow play materials from the Toy Library, as well as books from the Children's Centre and local library, to encourage Josh's skills in watching, looking, touching and playing. It was noticeable that Josie increased in confidence enough to become actively involved with Josh, especially in talking to him and establishing a routine of care and play both indoors and outdoors. Josie was also encouraged to borrow things from the library besides books, such as DVDs and music. The group arranged a trip to the library with the children one afternoon and Josie went along to help as the Children's Centre needed adults to make the visit possible. She started to borrow books for free and found that the library was only five minutes walk from her home.

Josh was then offered a place at a nursery group called Tiny Tots which was held at the Children's Centre when he reached the age of two. This provided three funded sessions a week. The nursery staff visited Josh at home before he began and saw that the flat where he lived had very few toys. By this time, Josh's baby sister Charlotte had been born and there was an obvious problem for Josie in that she was caring for two children. This meant the emphasis that had been given to Josh in terms of play and learning was diminishing.

When Josh started at Tiny Tots he found it overwhelming as there were so many resources on offer for him to play with. Josie looked forward to a break from Josh who was going through a period of having tantrums and being aggressive towards Charlotte. After a period of settling in Josh became accustomed to the routines and the opportunity to play at Tiny Tots; in particular he enjoyed the outdoors and messy play. However, his communication skills were not well developed and an inability to gain attention and be understood by other children was causing him frustration.

The Speech and Language Therapist became involved in the process of assessing Josh, and both the early years practitioners and Josie were included in supporting his language by playing at home and at the Children's Centre. The result was that his communication gradually improved as did his behaviour. Josh's key worker began to talk to Josie when she came to collect him. She was always full of praise for Josh's achievements and Josie herself began to praise and encourage Josh. Josie was pleased with Josh's progress and found the idea of him having a record of what he did as a 'learning journey' easy to follow and a practical way of seeing what went on at the centre. Josie was always heartened by the things that he was doing and fascinated by the progress being documented in his learning journeys booklet. She told the practitioner that she could not believe so much could be achieved by his 'just playing'. She continued to try out toys from the toy library with Josh to see if he liked them. Josie and Josh began to play together and to enjoy more of one another's company. She also began to bring comments and pictures from home to put into the learning journey. She took Charlotte to a group called Family Time each week and learned that play did not have to involve expensive toys and that play dough could be made very cheaply in her own kitchen. She could also see how much Charlotte enjoyed playing with sand, water and different natural materials.

Josie was now pregnant with her third child. During the pregnancy, she and her partner separated and when the baby was born Josie struggled to manage the three children alone and became depressed. However, during home visits from the Children's Centre it was noticed there were more books and play materials at home and that the children were more

(Continued)

engaged with Josie than previously observed. There was also a new table in the kitchen where the family were now taking meals together.

When the new baby, Ben, was seven months old, Josie felt better and thought he was old enough to go to crèche while she took a training course at the Children's Centre. She completed a basic computer course and went on to achieve a literacy and numeracy GCSE. She asked to help at Tiny Tots again and became more confident in playing with the children, even suggesting ideas as to what they could do when planning for the sessions. She observed how the staff talked to the children and some of the strategies they used to encourage positive behaviour. She began to use these herself and found that the children responded to her. The Early Years Professional in the Children's Centre noticed this and spoke to the Adult Learning Co-ordinator who suggested that Josie did an Introduction to Children's Play course. By this time, Josh was at infant school and Charlotte at preschool. Ben had just started Tiny Tots. The Adult Learning Co-ordinator was able to access funds for Josie to do an NVQ Level 2 in Childcare and Education based at the Children's Centre. During this, Josie looked at the centre's policies and was impressed to find a policy on play outlining how crucial staff at the centre thought play was for young children's learning and development.

When she received certificates for her courses the Children's Centre presented them in front of the children and they were each very proud of their mum. She helped at sports day and fun days and on trips out. The centre had in-service training days and twilight training sessions which Josie joined, developing her knowledge and understanding of child development. She noticed that the staff in the Children's Centre treated it as a learning community where everybody from the smallest child to the manager was continuously learning. This gave her the confidence and reassurance that nobody would judge her on her lack of knowledge or experience.

When Ben, her third child, was three and at nursery, Josie talked to the Adult Learning Co-ordinator who thought she was ready to start looking beyond the Children's Centre and introduced her to the local Further Education College, where Josie started an Access Course. The Job Centre Plus Journeys to Work Advisor at the centre was able to help Josie access the necessary benefits and grants to help with childcare and living costs.

Josie has now started a Teacher Training Course at university. The children are all at school and she feels that without the Children's Centre and the care, concern and encouragement of the staff, she would not have been able to achieve this. She is looking forward to the day when she can earn her own living and may be able to move to new accommodation with a garden for the children. She has a renewed confidence that Josh, Charlotte and Ben will achieve in school, aspire to better education and employment opportunities, build stronger peer relationships, be more self-confident and have higher self-esteem. Without building positive relationships between Josie and the professionals within the Children's Centre she may not have aspired to or achieved the goals that she now actively works towards.

The Role of Play in Supporting Positive Relationships

Mandy Andrews

Chapter Objectives

This chapter explores the interrelationship between play and developing positive relationships in child/child and adult/child inter-actions. It uses the voices of researchers and commentators that have been drawn from work spanning a number of decades to consider the need for a 'secure base' to support children in developing social and emotional strength and independence. It examines the way in which parents and carers are sometimes faced with issues which raise personal emotional needs that may need to be supported and addressed by practitioners in order to enable positive relationships to develop between the child, their parents, and the subsequent relationship with the setting.

The importance of a secure base

An important observation about children's play is that 'very early play is part of developing social relationships' and moreover that ' … the precursors of the things we call play have their origin in early social relationships' (Lewis, 1997: 24). What Lewis draws attention to is that play not only has a role in supporting social development in children but that it is also reliant upon strong social relationships underpinning the experiences of young children to give them the confidence and freedom to 'play'. This is because play, for children, is an intrinsically motivated exploration of the world around them and this includes exploring social worlds and relationships with and between other people. Lewis considers that children learn about social worlds earlier than object worlds, but it is the role of a key caregiver to take steps to direct the infant towards exploring external object worlds. Therefore very early play is reliant upon positive relationships and play serves the purpose of being both a part of social relationships and a tool for exploring the environment.

Trevarthen (2005: 1) has argued that infants mimic the social actions of others in an 'intuitive readiness to move rhythmically with others in games of Sociability'. Children are driven to build relationships and are able to communicate and form reciprocal bonds from a very young age. Babies will mimic adult movements perhaps before they are consciously in control of their physical actions and will usually be rewarded by a positive response from a caring adult. Think, for example, of how a child will form an accidental smile and be rewarded by a positive reaction in return. Reddy and Trevarthen (2004) argued that children as young as four months are consciously able to make gestures and facial expressions in order to invite both caregivers and strangers to 'play'. Such signal and response cycles lead to the development of early social relationships with significant others (usually the mother) who provides affirmation for the infant. This relationship supports wider exploration and social development as the child grows. In order to play with confidence a child must be confident that they will be supported in their play and should not expect indications of failure, rejection or humiliation from those close relationships. Bowlby (1988) has argued that children with 'secure relationships' with a mother or father are most likely to be confident and competent in their exploration of both cognitive and social situations now and in future. He suggests positive relationships with others, which he termed 'emotional bonds between individuals', are developed by the child by utilising working models of him or her self. In turn models of self or self-awareness are developed in part through affirmative actions by others, i.e. the positive feedback received from people around them. Ainsworth (1969) also found that those children most securely 'attached' (having a stable, fair, social relationship with the main carer) are most likely to be confident in their subsequent self-directed explorations. In contrast she also identified that children insecurely attached are more likely to show great anxiety in a range of forms when they are separated from their parent or carer. Trevarthen (2005) challenges such theories of attachment as limiting a concept of a child's requirement for adult support. He argues instead that children are programmed to desire reciprocal 'dialogues' playfully exploring and co-constructing a social context for development. However, what each of the above do agree on is that positive relationships are important for both play and the development of future social skills. Positive social relationships between the primary carer and child are essential to both positive play and future positive relationships with others as the child grows and develops.

Winnicott (1971) highlights the importance of a sense of self in developing social relationships. He argues that a responsive mother's face is a 'precursor to a mirror' and plays a vital part in creating a positive environment for self-awareness in the infant which can then support developing relationships with others. Winnicott argues that for babies the environment and 'self' are perceived together and it is only gradually that the infant can develop a separation of 'me' from 'not me', a sense of self and 'others'. A key part of this process is confidence and understanding from the infant that they will be 'held in mind' by the significant caregiver even when they are not present (Winnicott, 1971: 176). It is inevitable that at some point children will separate from their parent or carer and demonstrate a growing self-reliance as they explore with increasing independence. In time they learn to leave their secure base. If this 'holding' sense is secure, the emotional 'affect' of the child is balanced. This means that children's capacity to explore their concrete environment and personal emotions can develop. In the case study we are given glimpses of the way in which Josie supports Josh's sense of self by recognising his emotions and building an early positive relationship through paying him attention when he explores the treasure basket materials. His play alongside his mother enables him to understand he is different, but still emotionally linked to others, and that he can have control over other 'things' as he manipulates them to make noises or achieve other ends via his own choices. These are important foundations for developing positive relationships later in life.

Although Josh needs a stable relationship to develop through play, it is important to recognise that parenting is not always straightforward and sometimes there are various pressures on the ideal development of consistent and positive relationships between parens and children. One such pressure, for example, may be the arrival of siblings, as Josh experienced, who are demanding that sense of self-importance in their actions and relationships with others. Josh then has to adjust his understanding of self in relation to others and may be observed doing this through a concrete arrangements of dolls and other toys used to symbolise the different relationships. Self-concept is an important aspect of developing social relationships with others and Josie needs to take care to ensure that Josh's sense of self is maintained, perhaps through playful mimicry and praise. However, in the case study there are some issues which have the potential to restrict his development and self-concept, leaving him insecure in the nursery environment and potentially restricting his ability to communicate. Josie struggled with her own personal issues of low self-esteem which she gradually addressed through accessing opportunities for personal development. She also faced the pressure of poverty, poor social relationships with her partner, and three young children requiring attention. Such a struggle can present challenges for parents in building positive relationships to support self-reliant play. Perhaps Josie just lacked sufficient time to focus on Josh's identity needs or perhaps she was influenced by her own experiences of being parented. Fraiberg et al. (1975) wrote of 'Ghosts in the Nursery', which referred to the impact of past experiences of being parented and on an adult's ability to parent. It is possible that Josie's low self-esteem came from her own experiences of being challenged to succeed and criticised for failure and as a result she may have struggled to support Josh's self-esteem in a positive way. The play sessions promoted by the Children's Centre were in part intended to address these issues and to introduce a recognition of parent's achievements and affirmation rather than criticism.

Non-directive play strategies

In the case study Josie is supported in developing a strong and playful relationship with her son through attending the Children's Centre and learning non-directive play strategies. Non-directive play is when the adult does not take a lead role and 'direct' the purpose of the play but follows the child's lead and restricts their own involvement. Such play is both empowering and affirming for the child because they have control of the situation. At these sessions Josie was encouraged to find ways to play and learn with Josh and to understand how her positive and caring influence would help him to understand the world around him and improve their social interactions. She learned to mirror what Josh was doing when he played and put into words Josh's actions and behaviours as an affirming acknowledgement, for example by saying 'You are really banging those tins together aren't you!'. The supportive tone of her voice encouraged Josh to continue playing. Using guidance from skilled practitioners Josie was encouraged to develop her understanding of Josh's play. She learned to communicate positively with him, laughing and praising his actions, and supporting his social skills through modelling turn taking, showing positive regard, and making overt eye contact, as well as understanding and responding to his cues. Her developing understanding of his interests and abilities provided a reciprocal reward for her and positive affirmation for him. They shared emotional responses and actions and it was evident that their social developmental journeys were very much entwined.

One of the non-directive play strategies used by the Children's Centre to support positive relationships between parent and child is the use of treasure baskets, a form of heuristic play. Heuristic play, promoted by Eleanor Goldschmied and widely adopted in work with very young children, identifies both the capacity of children to know their desires and wants and to express these through play objects. She recognises that children possess a drive to explore objects beyond their current understanding (Goldschmied and Jackson, 2004). She suggests that young children enjoy exploring different textures, shapes, sounds and the consequences of their actions on a range of objects made available to them in an easily accessible box or basket. Goldschmied and Jackson explain that natural objects are particularly important for heuristic play and treasure baskets should contain a range of household and other objects, such as wooden spoons, small saucepans, pegs, chains, pastry brushes and nail brushes; fir cones and other 'found' natural objects are also relevant (all assessed for age appropriate use and safety). Goldschmied research identifies that children will quite happily explore a range of objects, their properties and concepts (such as solid, hollow, soft, hard, loud and quiet) with concentration and perseverance for some time. She also recognises that heuristic play has great importance as a medium for enabling expression in young children and is an integral part of children's social development.

Josh's play with treasure baskets may seem a solitary activity and not particularly one which would lead to social interaction, but in fact he is developing his sense of self and control over objects. He is exploring his ability to manipulate objects external to himself and consequently developing his sense of 'self' and 'other' as distinct concepts. This could be further supported by the inclusion of a mirror to the contents of the basket. His sister, Charlotte, may also be expressing her desires and needs through play when she shows great interest in sand play – she is developing an interest in playing with small world figures, hiding some and playing out in an almost therapeutic way her current understanding of relationships and links between people.

Heuristic play is empowering for children as the adult role is one of gently facilitating interaction and not overt involvement and there is no pressure on the child to 'achieve'. The adult has an opportunity to sit back and observe rather than intervene and lead with prompts and questions. It is much easier to see children's actions and expressions of need in a positive light when adults are more distant from their exploratory behaviour. In the case study Josie has opportunities to observe how Josh explores through play. With support from the practitioners she recognised his interests, the sounds he made and the concepts he was exploring. Goldschmied and Jackson (2004) as well as Whalley (2007) would argue that this helps an adult to understand children's individual motivations and behavioural drives. The 'ceaseless noise' made by Josh banging things together in the kitchen at home that had become frustrating to Josie (a tired parent who did not understand it's purpose) thus became a recognised exploration of cause and effect by her child. Given space to focus on her child at play she recognised and developed a fascination in Josh's growing ability to control something of the environment around him. Consequently a greater understanding began to develop between the two parties in the relationship. Goldschmied and Jackson (2004) wrote extensively about understanding that very young children are indeed 'people' capable of independent action, not merely dependent upon the given care of others. You may recall that Josie was amazed by the way that Josh could make his preferences known at a very young age by choosing from a range of materials.

Through play children learn and practise many social skills and heuristic play in a group situation supports peer-peer social relationships. Studies have found that children, even at a very young age, will actually be aware of the actions of those around them and echo these actions (Parten, 1933; Vygotsky, 1966; Karmiloff-Smith, 1994). In the case study Josie met with other parents at Family Time sessions and in greeting others started to provide a template for interaction that Josh would pick up and assimilate into his own play and development. Similarly, children exploring in proximity to others will copy behaviours they have seen, such as putting into, turning upside down, or throwing, and will both mimic the lead behaviour and make verbal exclamations to each other. Josh explored his treasure basket alongside Imran who was slightly older than him and who was exploring concepts of banging and up and down motions. Josh explored and then paused to watch his neighbour. He picked up a wooden spoon and found a metal container similar to Imran's saucepan and a small measuring tin which he turned upside down and began to bang with enthusiasm. He let out an explanation of pleasure 'hey' in a clear recognition that he had achieved his intended outcome. Josh was operating in parallel to Imran, but then reached out to him for an element of interaction. Perhaps Imran also heard this sound and experienced some pleasure in having stimulated a positive behaviour in his peer? Very young children can certainly share play experiences in concrete ways and communicate their feelings. This reinforces play as a tool for the development of social relationships.

Social development

Although Josh seemed socially at ease he went through a period of having tantrums and being aggressive towards his younger sister, Charlotte around the time of starting Tiny Tots. Karmiloff-Smith (1994) reminds us that tantrums can be recognised as a positive development in children. A tantrum is the outward display of behaviour arising from growth in independence and a desire for self-determination in the child that here is in conflict with the needs of adults or others around them. A positive relationship at this age will have elements of conflict. At two years old Josh was not mature enough to know how to manage the emotions that arose from frustrations he experienced due to the impact on his family relationships of the arrival of his new baby sister. Josie did not have time to acknowledge all of these emotions, yet it was important that they were recognised as valid by 'others' around him. Bion (1962) identifies a role for parents and practitioners in 'containing' these emotions. 'Containment' is a process of acknowledging the feelings of others which may have arisen from seemingly unpredictable and unmanageable situations. Acknowledgement effectively provides a 'parking place' for these unmanageable feelings until a time when they can be addressed and perhaps managed. There may not be immediate solutions to the sources of anxiety as was the case for Josh, as his little sister was unlikely to suddenly disappear or bend to his will, but if Josie was able to 'contain' his feelings by acknowledging them, perhaps by saying 'You are frustrated by this today', then there would have been a potential relief to the anxiety. It would be acknowledged and Josh could continue in his development. In such 'containing' activities it is important also to remember that Josh would perhaps return and address the issues causing frustration at a later date when he was less anxious. Practitioners at Tiny Tots later observed Josh expressing his frustration with a doll and role playing a busy parent. Through play Josh was working through some of his experiences and frustrations.

Containment draws on the social skill of empathy. This growing social skill can be seen in practice in children at play where elements of a shared experience can lead to positive relationships. Children as young as two years old can show signs of empathy with peers who demonstrate that they are hurt or who have a cut or graze. They may look at the cut or graze and say 'ouch', demonstrating a growing understanding of emotions in both self and others. To build relationships with others involves exploring their emotions and experiences, through the use of a growing understanding of 'self'. Jenkinson (2001: 47) emphasises how children will explore, perhaps with a play imitation of empathy, the very different thoughts, feelings and experiences of someone else. She cites a tale in which a girl with an artificial arm joins a nursery and other girls subsequently role play a situation in which one of them has no arms. Jenkinson concludes that through this play one of the girls was able to enter an alternative world to her own and came to know more about the new girl with the prosthetic limb through exploring what the concept meant to her. This role play was building empathy with a peer that would later build into a strong positive and supportive relationship.

Josie told Josh that he was 'so clever' when he was exploring the toys in the treasure basket and he gained a positive view of himself at that moment from the reassuring tone of her voice. Children in play will create safe environments for this exploration of self-image and a consequent growing understanding of others in relation to this concept of self. This understanding of self as similar to, but uniquely different from, others is a part of the process of developing relationships with others within a community of people. Josh was seen by his key worker acting out arguments between pretend mother and father figures in the home corner, sometimes taking the role of the father and directing his peers to say the words expressed by the 'mother'. In this way he was safely exploring through his play the very complex relationship issues within a family partnership. He would know more about himself at the end of his role play and also have a gauge for others.

Making transitions

Laevers (2000) recognises that for children to achieve in a setting they need strong positive relationship with the environment and a feeling that they are 'at home'. In the case study the practitioners in the Children's Centre worked hard to support Josh's transition into Tiny Tots, building his trust and ensuring familiar faces are around him. His key worker and mum supported him in this process of change through reassurance and surrounding him with familiar objects and toys from the Family Time sessions. Despite such efforts to support Josh's transition he still found the process difficult. He was overwhelmed by the stimulating environment and amount of resources, something he was not used to at home. This realisation challenged his sense of self in context, his wellbeing, and his ability to build positive relationships with others through an involvement in play. Josh once again needed to build a secure base from which to reach out and explore. Trevarthen (2005: 99) reminds us that around the middle of the second year ' ... a child has a fragile social identity, and is acutely aware of the potential difficulties of communicating with strangers'. He continues, 'it would appear that the imagination is reaching out to learn how other persons categorise their experiences but is sensitive to the risks of imitating without understanding'. Josh sought understanding but had difficulty communicating with his peers and was fearful of making those essential approaches necessary for communicating his need for play. Josh was not confident in his use of language and because he was not empowered through his attempts at communicating with his peers he became frustrated. He could not manage these feelings and did not have a firmly established positive relationship to 'contain' them. Consequently his behaviour erupted into regular tantrums in the Tiny Tot sessions. His key worker 'held' and 'contained' his frustrations through redirecting his behaviour to the home corner and modelling how he can play with other children. Over a period of time this helped him to become absorbed into the world of the nursery and to feel 'at home' once more.

Links with the EYFS

The concepts we have considered above, of holding, containment, and the secure base, are echoed in the principles of the EYFS. A key principle is that 'children learn to be strong and independent from a base of loving and secure relationships with parents and/or a key person' (DCSF, 2008f: 9). Josh had a good start with a secure relationship with his mother, but this deteriorated for a while when she was preoccupied with a new baby. The key worker strove to develop a new secure relationship with Josh as he began to attend nursery as she understood the need for a secure base to encourage his further exploration. The 'development matters' section of Personal, Social and Emotional Development, dispositions and attitudes in the EYFS tells us that at 16–26 months children should 'learn that they are special through the responses of adults' (DCSF, 2008e: 24).

The EYFS expands upon the principle of the secure base and

emphasises the need for positive relationships and a positive regard, or respect, for the child. The EYFS tells us that 'commitments are focused around respect; partnership with parents ... and the role of the key person' (DCSF, 2008f: 9). Josh was shown respect from both Josie and his key worker. Such respect affirmed his sense of self and his understanding of his own abilities and actions and once again positive relationships formed the basis for play and learning. Josie in turn experienced a partnership with the setting which helped her to form positive relationships with Josh. This supported children 'having a positive self-image and showing that they are comfortable with themselves' (DCSF, 2008e: 38).

The EYFS also recognises the value of wellbeing for an exploration of self-awareness and self-direction. Within the EYFS area of learning and development relating to Personal Social and Emotional Development it is a requirement that 'providers must ensure support for children's emotional well-being to help them to know themselves and what they can do' (DCSF, 2008e: 12). This area of learning also includes the goal that children will 'have a developing awareness of their own needs, views and feelings and be sensitive to the needs, views and feelings of others' (DCSF, 2008e: 12), but that they will also be confident to initiate new ideas, speak in a familiar group, express their needs, and select and use activities and resources independently. These are all aspects of play behaviour, but are ones which are dependent on early strong relationships. It is the practitioner's role to ensure that children's sense of self (their baseline measure for exploration) is strong. It is also important that children feel secure, or 'at home' in the setting, building positive relationships with key adults to enable greater exploration. After all, undertaking challenging play for social development is hard work.

Continuing Professional Development Activity

This chapter has considered the EYFS principle Positive Relationships. It has identified that heuristic play is one way of developing such relationships between children and between adults and children. It should not be seen as the sole province of young children, but can also be developed with older children by using containers of small toys, shells, jewellery and other items worthy of exploration and experimentation. Exploring these types of materials in a group environment will also stimulate children's communication and imagination. You may provide opportunities for children's play in the same way, but not recognise it as heuristic play. This CPD activity will help you think about the ways in which you can provide play opportunities for building positive relationships.

Play for positive relationships

Aims

- To consider how you can provide play opportunities for building positive relationships in child/child and child/adult interactions.

- To consider the 'theory and processes' involved in promoting heuristic play and how these can be transferred into your setting to build on the EYFS principle of positive relationships.

- To think about what you might observe when children play and to understand the theory introduced in this chapter about playing, learning and forging positive relationships.

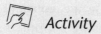 ## Activity

1 In small groups or pairs, list the various play opportunities that children engage with in your setting which you believe support building positive relationships. What components of play ensure that it is building a positive interaction?

2 How do you know if you have seen positive relationships develop?

3 Think about your role in children's play – do you believe that children can build their own positive relationships without your support? List some examples of occasions when you have seen children do this.

4 Now consider how you provide for heuristic and treasure basket play. Discuss the following:

5 How do you define your area for heuristic play, do you set boundaries or have a particular play area?

6 How do you promote social interaction between children, adults and the environment. It may be that you have ideas and objects which span all of these. Think of the resources you provide and how they promote:

- actions relating to self-awareness;

- actions relating to control of the environment;

- communication and exclamations indicating achievement and affirmation;

- children's communications with each other.

7 How might you further extend play opportunities in your setting to build on these skills?

8 Identify areas of your practice where the theory and processes introduced in this chapter match what you do and what you believe in terms of developing positive relationships for children.

Question to consider

- *How will the discussions you have engaged in through this activity inform and support your practice?*

This activity has asked you to consider how you support and build positive relationships with children through play opportunities. The chapter and CPD activity has advocated for heuristic play which you may already make provision for in your setting. You now need to think about how engaging in discussion will help you to reflect on and inform you practice. It may be that you will want to take some of the ideas and try these out, or you might want to analyse your actions and interactions with children more closely. It is important that the activity is not seen in isolation, but that you examine your discussions in relation to your underlying values and beliefs and check whether these are apparent through your practice.

 ## Summary

This chapter has explored and reviewed the voices of commentators who have researched and studied play and learning. They suggest that play is something which is complex and interrelated to many other facets of child development. This is articulated through the words of Froebel who argued that play ' ... is the highest expression of human development in childhood, for it alone is the free expression of what is in the child's soul. It is the purest and most spiritual product of the child and at the same time it is a type and copy of human life at all stages and in all relations' (cited in Jenkinson, 2001: 50). The chapter has sought to understand this perspective by considering social relationships, the importance of parents, significant others, and the 'social community' the child inhabits. It has also attempted to convey the message that play enables a child to act out understandings of how others behave and also how they behave.

5

Parental Partnerships

Michael Reed and Rosie Walker

> **Chapter Objectives**
>
> This chapter examines why parent partnerships are an important aspect of early years provision. It explores research into parental involvement looking at the benefits and challenges of working with parents to promote children's play and learning. It also explores how practitioner's values can support collaboration and partnership, arguing that play, children's learning and positive parenting go hand in hand. It examines how settings work towards partnership and considers the challenges of moving beyond collaboration through supporting integrated services in order to develop a shared understanding of play.

Collaboration or partnership?

One of the aims of *Every Child Matters* (ECM) (DfES, 2004) is to integrate and co-ordinate services to improve the experiences and outcomes for children and their families. At the heart of this is communication in working towards the same aims and shared values of what is important for children. *Every Child Matters* led to the creation of structures which promote the integration of services provided by those agencies concerned with representing collaborative and multi-agency working. This development has had a transformative effect on the concept of professionalism for the early years workforce and has also provided a focus on the value of co-operating and collaborating with parents. It has moved towards ensuring that early years practitioners deliver childcare and education which reflects the significance of building partnerships with parents to provide a holistic view of children's lives. Within the EYFS it is now a requirement for practitioners to consult with parents (DCSF, 2008e: 6) and allow children to 'benefit from a single play based framework for learning, development and care' (DCSF, 2009a: 12). Partnership with parents is also seen as an important part of the inspection process (OfSTED, 2008) and is a significant focus for Quality Improvement programmes in England. Here quality is seen as reflecting 'partnership with parents/carers, children, other settings and partner professionals to support children's learning and development' (DCSF, 2008h: 6). This clearly suggests a shift towards a holistic approach to achieving positive outcomes for children. It also acknowledges the influence of the family in shaping children's experiences.

Within the EYFS there is less practical advice as to what effective partnership with parents might look like. It refers to the importance of supporting children's development and the role of the key person but given the central importance of play-based practice there is limited guidance addressing how a practitioner can extend play outside of the setting and into other areas of children's lives. Perhaps because of this, parental support in practice may not focus on the integrated play and learning which should be emphasised within a setting and consequently parental relationships appear more like collaboration (working together) rather than partnership (having a relationship and dialogue working towards the same aims). For this to happen there needs to be a clear understanding of what is meant by play and a need for parents to understand what this means. Parents may well want to hear about and be involved in what children are doing during their day, they may take an interest and have a positive relationship with a setting, but this is more likely to evolve into collaboration based on the strategies of good communication, unless there is a genuine desire to explain, promote and recognise that play is important for children's development and that it straddles what goes on in the setting and the home. Play can be used as a way to move forward from collaboration to partnership by engaging parents in a meaningful dialogue about what children are demonstrating and developing through their play and asking parents to consider if their child engages in similar play contexts at home. In the case study Josie began to make better connections with practitioners when she attended regular Family Time sessions and started to build a relationship with Josh's key person. As Josie's understanding about Josh's behaviour in play improved, she felt more confident in asking questions and trying out suggestions by the practitioner's at home. Through feeding back what she had observed and learned about Josh with practitioners at the Children's Centre they began to take small steps towards partnership working.

Parental partnership requires a professional perspective which sees parents as part of a child's development and avoids what Moss et al. (2007) see as a cultural expectation in promoting learning strategies and outcomes rather than developing the relationships which underpin these. He identifies these relationships as active participation within communities and between practitioners and parents to understand and support children's play and learning processes. In the case study Josie started to engage in this process by attending the Children's Centre and accessing their sessions. She was drawn to the centre because of her needs but the centre was also reaching out to her by developing links with the local community. Gasper (2010) acknowledges how important this can be and argues that it moves away from the accepted model that people will want to and should indeed access services. It illustrates a professional change in philosophy and action towards community support.

Changing perspectives: the value of parental partnerships

A comprehensive review of research on the benefits for children's wellbeing and learning when practitioners, parents and children work as an effective team comes from Desforges and Abouchaar (2003), who suggest that what parents 'do' with their children is highly significant in terms of their development, education and emotional wellbeing. They argue that this should not be limited to planned activities, outings or new experiences, but also involves everyday engagement and interaction, for example:

- having meal times around a table and encouraging children's conversation;

- actively involving children in day-to-day tasks such as tidying up or helping look after a pet;

- developing and building on new learning experiences, such as planting flowers in the garden.

These examples are often considered as simple life experiences and taken for granted, but with the changing nature of the way in which family life is organised they can be overlooked in preference for more immediate priorities. The report 'Every Parent Matters' (DCSF, 2007b) considers the way that family life is altering and how professionals need to respond to the different dynamics of modern day parenting. Parents or carers may work long hours with children having greater opportunities to keep themselves occupied through television or computer games: as a result in general a convenience culture has emerged to enable families to carry out their busy and diverse lives. This may mean a less meaningful engagement between parents and children and require practitioners to provide guidance, and sometimes intervention, to support families in accessing play and learning opportunities. The case study provides a useful example of how Josie benefited from a wide range of professionals concerned with her childrens learning and development. This ultimately helped her to learn and develop the same skills she wanted her children to have, for example:

- developing positive relationships with others;

- becoming more confident and self-assured;

- making friends;

- having a positive attitude and outlook;

- being able to express needs and preferences;

- valuing the freedom to play as a process for independent learning.

As a practitioner you will need to consider the ways in which you provide opportunities to engage with parents in your setting. This could be through the policies and practices of your own setting and perhaps also through the informal networks you establish by being part of a local community. It is important to reflect on whether brief but regular contact is enough to ensure parents understand what you are trying to achieve via your setting's underpinning values and ethos in relation to play. Josie's example in the case study demonstrates how important it is for practitioners to see the connections between what happens at home and what happens in the setting so they can provide tailored support for Josie and her family. This relies on practitioners developing their own skills in understanding the progressive value of play and working with others, as well as making links with other professionals who support families.

Research has shown that young children achieve more and are happier when practitioners work together with parents and share ideas about how to support and extend children's learning (Athey, 1990; Meade, 1995). The DCSF (2007b) argue that practitioners need to establish active and equal relationships with parents to build trust and move beyond collaboration and towards partnership. In building these relationships they recognise that parents and children have rights which should be respected when working with individual families. The parental partnership can be difficult and complex, but the DCSF (2007b) put forward that parents are children's first educators and that in establishing positive relationships early years professionals can support the knowledge and understanding of parents in the value of play, learning and development. In working towards establishing a culture of partnership in your setting, you will naturally begin to support developing positive expectations of involvement, commitment and communication from parents.

In working towards achieving these values an emphasis is placed on dialogue between parents and practitioners to support seamless opportunities to foster learning in both the home and early years setting. Parents are encouraged to spend time observing their children play and to see their role as responding to their child's preferred style of playing, being and learning. Bruce (2001) stresses how important play is for the developing child and argues that children use play to bring together what they know into a connected and whole way, where experiences can be sculpted by the child and also extended throughout the setting or home environment. In the same way developing relationships with parents in understanding this perspective is important so they can begin to value the significance of play in contributing to their child's development. The theme of 'positive relationships' within the EYFS is based upon the principle that a secure rapport with parents and/or a key person enables children to play and learn to be independent. It emphasises the need for practitioners to develop ways of working with parents in order to underpin the value of supporting play dispositions and of helping parents to understand how children become interested and motivated to learn (DCSF, 2008e). One way to develop this relationship is to share observations of children's play in terms of the experiences and processes children have engaged in rather than focus on outcome-based activities. This supports parents in developing an understanding of how you support children and what they are doing when they play. This dialogue creates the capacity for parents and practitioners to recognise each other's value base and also to discuss different perspectives, approaches and practices to support children's play.

Developing practice

The Early Learning Partnership Project (ELPP) is an example of national partnership working which targets 'hard to reach' and vulnerable parents of children between one and three years of age through a range of approaches to encourage them to be involved in activities that can support the early learning of their children. A particular focus is placed on the parents of children who have been identified as being at risk of a learning delay. This project was set up in 2006 to test out various ways of encouraging parents in disadvantaged families to become involved with their children and their interests. Nine voluntary organisations examined 12 different approaches between October 2006 and March 2008. The evaluation found that the project gave parents 'new skills, techniques and creative ideas' and 'new confidence in their role as educators', but it also found there was no improvement in parenting behaviour that challenged children's thinking or extended their communication skills (Evangelou et al., 2008: ii). The project also focussed on ways to improve the skills of the early years workforce, including volunteers, so they could better engage with parents to support children. It recognised the need for professional development to build up practitioner's skills in order to support parents and suggested strategies to improve communication and positive relationships. Coe et al. (2008) also researched parents who had been described as 'hard to reach' and considered various factors affecting the ability of four SureStart programmes to engage with families in a multicultural city. They found there were significant numbers of eligible families not accessing SureStart services because while many held a positive view of the programme, they also harboured a number of serious misconceptions about what it provided. Problems were compounded by other pressures such as social isolation and difficulty in accessing SureStart services. The findings suggested that contacting parents early, before misconceptions arose, and establishing and maintaining positive relationships were important in increasing parental engagement.

Siraj-Blatchford (2007: 13) suggests that supporting parents to meet their children's needs and developing practitioner's skills are 'two sides of the same coin'. She argues that the way children develop though play and find meaning as part of their engagement with the real world is through effective practice being applied in early years settings. This involves the provision of supportive yet challenging play environments and a parental ability to develop gradually more sophisticated communication and collaboration strategies in partnership with children and parents. The Effective Provision of Pre School Education (EPPE) project also found that settings were most effective when there was shared communication between parents and practitioners on subjects such as day-to-day routines and activities (Siraj-Blatchford and Sylva, 2004). However, individual practitioners can sometimes feel unsure and threatened when talking with parents as much as parents may experience hesitance and feel overawed by those professionals who work with their children.

Consequently, a reciprocal relationship is important so practitioners and parents can both focus on meeting children's needs. The Key Elements of Effective Practice (KEEP) project suggests practitioners need knowledge, the ability to develop a practical response to the needs of parents in the community, and the ability to collaborate with other professionals in order to understand and build on their skills in developing confidence to facilitate positive relationships with parents (DfES, 2005b).

From these examples it is clear that working in partnership with parents requires you to demonstrate a range of professional dispositions, such as perseverance, reflective thinking and the ability to challenge assumptions. In the case study the Children's Centre practitioners demonstrated some of these skills through working together to support Josie and her children. They used their knowledge and expertise to help and more importantly to bring together a range of professional experiences to build up a picture of Josie's family and provide a multi-agency approach to support their immediate and ongoing needs. You may not work in a situation where integrated services are available, but you will need to know about the agencies available in your area, where they are located, their role, and your role as part of a shared approach to provision. Consequently, McInnes (2007) states that having a knowledge and understanding of all this is crucial when working for the individual needs of a child and building positive relationships with a family. Central to this must be the value that you place on play and how you advocate this to parents and other professionals. Josie's story is an example of the 'Positive Relationships' principle that embraces the complex work that practitioners do on a daily basis and is an integral part of the EYFS. Practitioners were alert to the early signs of Josie and her children's needs and by responding appropriately and sensitively, and engaging and encouraging her over time, they enabled her to make a positive contribution to her local community and beyond.

The Children's Centre approach is to focus on what they can contribute to families rather than expecting the family to have the ability to search out and somehow just access the services available. This goes some way to enabling children and families to overcome the barriers to participation and learning. In the case study, Josie's story shows the time it can take for parents to build trust in practitioners and effective communication to develop. It demonstrates the importance of all families being welcomed, as well as having their needs recognised and accommodated as they take ownership of and shape the services they require. However, there is a fine dividing line between providing support and creating a professional dependency.

Carefully managed and co-ordinated services will have this in mind and in the case study this brought success by recognising that Josie had autonomy in making decisions about her children. The practitioners in the Children Centre balanced Josie's needs and the needs of Josh, Charlotte and Ben so they all felt included and valued.

Continuing Professional Development Activity

It is important to think not only about your values in working with parents but also about how you will remain up to date in your thinking and practice in relation to continuing positive relationships. Technology has increasingly become a part of everyday life and as such is used as a tool to keep practitioners informed of developments and changes in policy and practice by agencies and other organisations. Therefore it is necessary that you have the requisite skills to access this rich source of material and develop a critical awareness of its purpose and impact.

Web-based research: a focus on parents

Aims

- To develop an awareness of the material that is available via the internet on working with parents.

- To engage in critical reflection on the purpose and impact of internet sources.

- To share new knowledge with colleagues, considering the impact this has on your attitude towards working with parents.

This activity relies on your ability to access desktop computers or laptops. If you are organising this activity as part of structured CPD sessions you will need to ensure computers with internet access are available prior to starting the session to accommodate the number of people taking part. This may mean organising the activity so that everyone works in pairs or small groups around the number of computers you have or undertaking the activity within a specific time slot. This can have benefits such as sharing ICT skills and generating a discussion on the content and process of the activity. Alternatively, you could break the task down into manageable parts so each person can (over a period of time, for example a few days or a week) use their own ICT equipment to select a website to evaluate. Individuals can then report back to the CPD session in small groups or even distribute their views online.

 Activity

Access the websites listed below and evaluate the information you find, using the questions to help structure your thoughts and critical thinking.

Purpose of the website

- What are the objectives of the website or the research on which it is reporting?

- Why has this website been created?

- For whom will the information be useful?

Ways of communicating

- Is the website easy to use and understand?

- What are the key points the website is making?

- Where has the information come from?

- Is it based on research with parents and families?

- How old is the information?

- Who publishes on or contributes to the website?

- Is it fair and unbiased? Is it speaking to the intended audience?

Reflect on the quality of the content of the websites and how valuable this activity is for developing your practice and relationships with parents.

Recommendations

- Why would/wouldn't you recommend someone else to visit this site?

- What information resonates with your professional philosophy and experience of working with parents?

- How might you use what you have read/found out in your practice?

- What are the positive/negative aspects of the information you have found?

- Having done all this, where would you store the information so that others can use it and in what form?

- Are there any websites that contain comparable or conflicting material, research or advice?

The sites

Start by considering some websites that have been established with government funds or through government agencies. These are likely to still be available (though perhaps not with exactly the same information or emphasis, as times change) and should be around for some time.

- *The Parenting Academy*

  www.parentingacademy.org/

  This is the new National Academy for Parenting Practitioners and parenting support courses.

- *National Standards*

  www.nationalstrategiescpd.org.uk/

  This site contains resources about parents as partners in early learning and DVDs about play and learning. There is also information about parents as partners, case studies, links to the Family and Parenting Institute and forums for discussion.

- *The University of Warwick*

  www.schoolsnetwork.org.uk

  The university has recently published the results of its year-long study of over 100 parental involvement projects. The results reinforce the importance of parental engagement where parents and teachers work together to improve learning.

- *PEAL Project*

  www.peal.org.uk

  The aim of this project is to support practitioners in encouraging and developing parental involvement in children's early learning. The project – Parents, Early Years and Learning (PEAL) – has produced training and resource materials based on the key elements of authentic relationships, communication and partnership. The PEAL reader, which accompanies this site, includes clear guidance on reinforcing training and helping to establish practitioner confidence in working in partnership with parents.

- *PEEP Project*

  www.peep.org.uk

  The Peers Early Education Partnership (PEEP) aims to contribute towards a significant improvement in educational attainment by whole communities of children, from their birth, by working with parents and carers.

- *Children's Workforce Development Council (CWDC) – Common Core and the Functional Map*

  www.cwdcouncil.org.uk/common-core

  The CWDC have been working to promote the Common Core of Skills and Knowledge (DfES, 2005b) which are six things that the government want the early years workforce to show in their practice. More recently, the Children's Network has produced an additional 'map' that sets out the roles, responsibilities and skills required of an early years professional.

- *Literacy Trust*

www.literacytrust.org.uk

This site argues that the earlier parents become involved in their children's literacy practices, the more profound the results and the longer-lasting the effects. It stresses that early intervention is crucial and that learning starts from within the context of the family. Take a look at this site for valuable resources which include research evidence and materials for very young children and babies. Different pages on this site include:

Child development

www.literacytrust.org.uk/talktoyourbaby/researchindex1.html

Research reports

www.literacytrust.org.uk/Research/earlyindex.html

Practical examples of how to involve parents in reading

www.literacytrust.org.uk/earlyreadingconnects/Family/index.html

Family involvement toolkit

www.literacytrust.org.uk/earlyreadingconnects/family_involvement_toolkit.pdf

Early reading

www.literacytrust.org.uk/earlyreadingconnects/gettingstarted.html

Database of articles and news about parental involvement, recent government and research reports

www.literacytrust.org.uk/Database/parentupdate.html

Questions to consider

- *What are you going to do with the information you have found?*

You may use the activity above to update your knowledge of working with parents, to confirm what you already know or as a way to develop your critical thinking. Whatever your choice, it is important for you to see the links between the thinking behind research at a national level, such as government strategies and how these impact on your day-to-day practice. You may wish to disseminate information to your team or plan further CPD activities based on what you have discovered. Crucially it is vital that you do not feel overwhelmed by the mass of information available, and sometimes contradictory advice. In such a situation you will need to apply your values and beliefs about working with parents and consider how useful the information you have sourced is for your future practice. You may find it helpful to relate back to the questions at the beginning of the activity to help you think about a critical approach to how you use internet resources.

- *How do you keep up to date with new developments in policy?*

Some of the websites in this activity may be familiar and some you may be accessing for the first time. It is worth considering which style of website you prefer, as you are more likely to return to those that are easy to navigate and maintain your interest. Think about the strategies you will implement to ensure you revisit these websites. This may mean signing up to an email alert or adding a page to your favourites list. You may want to task certain members of your team who are skilled ICT users and enjoy surfing the internet to share updates at regular team meetings, or you may recognise that using the internet is an overall skill that needs to be addressed.

▢ Summary

This chapter has only provided a 'snapshot' of the kind of evidence available on parental involvement in play-based practice. It has illustrated the importance given to this subject by the considerable number of parental partnership projects and initiatives either designed by Local Authorities or commissioned by the government, that are currently operating in the UK. The research can sometimes be ambiguous, but it does still seem to support the value that is given to parental collaboration and partnership which is contained within the EYFS. What is also clear is the increasing responsibility that is placed upon practitioners to actually implement these initiatives. You are now being asked to become aware of your values and approaches that support play as a means to extend and develop learning. You must also have the ability to communicate with parents and carers, so that they too may understand the progressive value of play in the early years.

Making Connections between Home, the Setting and Key Workers

Sue Callan with Carole Ellis and Helen Richards

Chapter Objectives

This chapter builds on the underlying themes and strategies emerging from supporting unique qualities, enabling environments, and learning and development. It examines the possibilities of home visits in supporting children and families through the development of positive play relationships and recognises how this enables learning and development to emerge for all involved. The terms 'home visitor', 'outreach practitioner' and 'family support worker' have been used interchangeably in recognition of the interconnectedness of skills and attributes of early years professionals and the chapter explores how Family Support Workers contribute to the themes and principles of EYFS, as well as community development and multi-professional aspects of *Every Child Matters* (DfES, 2004).

Making connections in play

In the quest to build positive relationships between children and adults a fundamental ingredient is mutual respect. Achieving this is sometimes a difficult journey, but some of the underlying principles include engaging with the child's voice and allowing them to express their ideas and opinions so they feel listened to within a meaningful context (Clark and Moss, 2001). This is essential in play where the child has a sense of autonomy and the freedom to invite an adult, be this a parent, home visitor or practitioner, into the play on their own terms. Donaldson (1992) and Rogoff (1990) developed the notion of an adult play 'partner', where the adult facilitates the child to follow their own play agenda but also supports them in scaffolding their learning such as in communication or negotiation (Smidt, 2009). In this sense what adults do when they are involved in children's play is crucial: finding the balance of interaction and understanding the importance of play and the impact of their actions are part of building up that mutual respect.

Viewing parental and community participation in play, especially in the home environment, provides a context for supporting alignment and continuity with the setting. Outreach workers are the conduit for this, supporting the child to continue their play in different environments, yet practise the same skills. This supports cognitive links with what they are doing and involves parents and practitioners in play because connections between the two involve placing the child at the centre of the process. However, this connection relies on a number of assumptions:

- the parent/carer is motivated to make links with the setting;

- the setting is developing positive relationships with the parents/carers so that a two-way dialogue is established;

- the setting uses play materials that parents/carers can access/replicate at home;

- the setting and parents/carers believe in the value of play and basing their practice around the child's needs;

- parents/carers will devote time to playing with the child;

- the culture of the setting and the home are based on the same principles.

Many relationships between the parent and setting will not have all of these elements in place, yet they can still make positive connections to support the interests of the child. Donaldson (1978) recognises that this is because beyond the daily routines of the setting the 'human context' for child and family learning is an important underlying value for practice. In your setting you may think this is not obvious, but do try to look for some of the following signs:

- children are welcomed and greeted on first name terms;

- displays focus on children's contributions and are at child height so they can see them;

- children are encouraged to share their experiences from home in order to support their learning and development;

- children have a sense of ownership over their play space;

- home traditions are integrated into daily practice rather than being 'bolted on'.

These qualities are very much valued in the early childhood curriculum approaches of New Zealand (Te Whariki) and a region of Italy (Reggio Emilia), which focus on the natural engagement between children, parents/carers and practitioners as part of the interaction of teaching and learning. Malaguzzi (1993) recognizes the importance and relevance of parents and professionals working together to promote curiosity, investigation, and a child's potential in the community.

The following observation from Family Time in a Children's Centre provides a good example of this and highlights the ways in which positive relationships are built using simple materials (a cardboard tube and lambswool duster) which could be made available in the home or setting. It focuses not only on play, but also on the connections between mother and child.

> Mum put the duster in the tube and made it pop out at the other end and tickle her baby's toes. She made the duster move fast and slow and said 'it's coming, it's coming, pop!' The baby watched his mother's face and then the end of the tube. His body became still as he waited for the action and then he laughed as the duster appeared and tickled his toes before disappearing again. As the game progressed the baby's anticipation became animated, with his feet jigging and his breath panting. The mother's efforts were rewarded with the baby's laughter which bubbled up from inside and was so infectious it attracted the attention of other parents who all enjoyed seeing this pair at play.

Judy Dunn's work with families (1984, 1986, and 1993) shows how babies build on early attachment relationships in order to engage positively with others and especially with siblings. This provides evidence of the strong communication and social skills of babies and toddlers. For example, in the extract the baby quickly understood the

game and what was going to happen. He anticipated the duster pop-
ping out of the tube from his mum's expression, her vocalisation,
and the time that lapsed between each appearance. Such play can be
initiated in a variety of contexts with a variety of adults or older children demonstrating the significance of play in supporting
developing relationships.

Principles and practice

Family support workers engage in partnership with parents and
other professionals to provide services with an emphasis on family
learning and community development. This ensures that the needs
both of individuals and the community are taken into consideration
to ultimately support the child in their learning and development
(Bronfenbrenner, 1979). This approach endeavours to underpin
frameworks such as the EYFS (DCSF, 2008e) and *Every Child Matters*
(DfES, 2004) which make strong reference to these principles.

However, general overarching statements made in the EYFS do not
address the complexities of providing support for children and families. Each child and family will have specific and diverse needs
requiring individual programmes and goals. Yet family support
teams also have to fulfil the formal requirements of the SureStart
Core Offer and Principles (DCSF, 2009b; see also DCSF and DoH,
2008) and where applicable the Portage codes of practice (White and
Cameron, 1987). Each month the multi-professional teams involved
in the community are required to record information about the 'tar-
get reach' (i.e. how many families they have reached and which
category they fall into: for example, new families, single parents,
young parents, fathers and ethnic minority families). It is necessary
to do this in order to secure future government funding for outreach
teams. As a result, outreach workers commonly recognise their role
as a supportive catalyst for wider social change, with discussion of
emotionally challenging aspects of the role explored as part of team
supervision and mentoring.

It is not unusual for outreach workers to be involved in facilitating
Family Time groups in Children's Centres. Such sessions were initially provided under the *Birth to Three Matters* framework in which
play is described as being key to development (DfES, 2002). *Every
Child Matters* (DfES, 2004) and the subsequent Children Act 2006
requirements are now contained within the EYFS (DCSF, 2008e). In
this respect, planning for sessions in the Children's Centre and at
home by the practitioner combines family learning and social inclu-

sion as a requirement of wider government policy aims. The sessions also offer support for families' health, parenting and learning and focus on promoting children's social and emotional development through play and education. Babies and toddlers learn to socialise and communicate in a safe and positive environment and parents have access to emotional support, friendships, and advice about health and parenting issues.

Sometimes, parents will need the support of practitioners to help them engage in providing play opportunities for their child. This was evident in the case study where initially Josie did not know how to support her first child, Josh, in play, or how to recognise the kinds of resources that would support his experiences and development. By providing opportunities for different types of play where parents can get involved with their children in the experience, the Children's Centre is scaffolding and supporting parenting skills in how to play with their children. This can be extended by discussion with outreach workers, i.e. practitioners who mainly work within the local community and visit families' homes. Callan and Morrall (2009) note the practitioner's role is vital in promoting the emotional well-being which influences *adults'* motivation, curiosity and willingness to explore and also the resilience to be able to deal with parents' experiences of playing with their child.

When parents are involved in their child's play they become more interested in how they can support their child's development. Keeping them involved is reliant on the co-operation of the family, the relationship with the practitioner, and the way in which they present and communicate information. If observations are kept by both parties, it is possible for parents to contribute their own views about their children's play experiences between home visits. The EYFS encourages this, but does not offer practical solutions on how it may be achieved. Observations do not have to be onerous but it is important that parents feel involved, so it is essential that they are consulted about how such observations are made and kept. A practical way to do this is by using a notebook where practitioners and parents both contribute through descriptions of the child's play. Equally photos, video or audio recordings could be included if standard formats are difficult for the family or may not be in their home language. In the same way, not all parents can respond to written instructions. From the case study we know that in the beginning Josie was developing her own literacy skills, but her participation in the recording process helped put the family experiences into a meaningful context. For other families the spoken word and modelling by the outreach worker may be more comfortable and valuable. An additional challenge may be that one parent may not always be at home and some of the core messages about the value of the play that has been planned for the child might be 'lost in translation'.

Integrated working enables the outreach practitioner to share information with other professionals working with the family. This helps the team around the child to complement and reinforce each other's work and ensures a consistent approach. By keeping a copy of observations and (where appropriate) development plans if the child has additional needs, the parent then has positive evidence of progress which they may find encouraging. Children with additional needs may also access Portage Services at home and in the setting where Portage workers can model specific instruction and activities. The child is taught a skill or offered opportunities to develop an emerging skill by using suggested strategies regularly. In this situation the practitioner has the opportunity to find out what happens in a usual family day to see if the routine offers natural opportunities for developing skills rather than having time set aside especially. These interactions may not initially be viewed as play, but considered instead as a way in which to engage children in basic skills to access play opportunities at a later stage. Essentially the home visiting team is committed to play-based pedagogy within which children's rights are paramount. If children present other outcomes, these are followed within play-based provision in order that action by the practitioner is consistent with child-led practice and planning in other contexts. Through a professional, relaxed, friendly approach, home visitors can act as a portal for parents to access other services available locally with the result that the long-term wellbeing of the child and family will be enhanced.

Working with families at home

Callan and Morrall (2009) present a template that might have enabled Josie to identify her areas of experience that require additional support whilst hopefully recognising some positive aspects. This could help Josie to maintain a feeling of control over her circumstances and engage in a constructive relationship with the home visiting team. Within good practice, any plans and goals for the children must be decided with Josie rather than prescribed for her. A 'contract' was established through open discussion so that Josie could understand that the one hour a fortnight contact, for example, would have a minimal effect if she could not sustain the play between visits.

In the case study Josie identified her priorities for the home visits as support for Charlotte to regain some of her independence skills, especially drinking out of a cup rather than depending on a bottle which had been a source of conflict. Josie also needed some idea of how she could stimulate and motivate the baby at home as she could not easily see how to apply the guided experiences from the Children's Centre. In this respect, much of the play that occured in the family home, as the result of a discussion with the practitioner, supported understanding and tolerance in the parent/child relationship.

Sometimes families can become so entrenched in routines, stress and negative feelings that the introduction of easily accessible fun can offer respite and an alternative coping mechanism. It could be argued that play performs a significant role in supporting and safeguarding the emotional development of the child within the family. Therefore, the decisions facing the practitioner and Josie about what type of play and how this can best be supported required sensitive negotiation. Communication about play strategies, backed by theory, was also important if Josie was to be convinced about the significance of play.

Building positive relationships through play

Although in the case study the relationship and trust established with Josie was good, the home visits only provided a brief snapshot of the family issues including, as the result of observations, the play needs of the child. This meant that collaborative, professional relationships were vital because they enabled the home visitor to address wider issues. The EYFS (2008e: 10) states the 'necessity and effectiveness of multi disciplinary communication' and the case study is an example of such interaction. Whilst facilitating the Family Time group at the Children's Centre, the outreach worker observed that Josie's second child, Charlotte, if provided with a cup for her drink, could swallow but not regulate the amount of liquid entering her mouth. It ran down her face, resulting in a soaking which was frustrating and uncomfortable, but she enjoyed playing with the resulting splashes on the table. The lack of independent skill in this area might have led to dehydration if it were not tackled long term and the practitioner shared her concern with Josie. They agreed that the unfamiliar, uncontrollable nature of liquid was at the route of the problem and explained Charlotte's preference for the bottle. They discussed whether the problem might be addressed through Charlotte's interest in water play.

Through engaging with the water tray at Family Time, Charlotte developed her skill in being able to transfer liquid from one container to another with less spillage and being able to cope with the shifting weight of liquid. When drinking from a beaker she was then be able to regulate the amount of liquid in her mouth so she did not get wet. Not only did these learning opportunities provide a sensory experience, they also bolstered her self-esteem and confidence and care for her dignity, which was part of the social and emotional component of the EYFS concept of making a Positive Contribution (DCSF, 2008e). It also began to 'repair' her relationship with Josie as they had begun to establish negative responses to each other around food and drinking. Charlotte was able to access water play independently and voluntarily alongside her peers and an emerging schema was identified in her repeated filling and pouring game. Seeing how the other children played enables her to experience the support that simple social play offered and she began to share and interact with other children engaged in the same play. Generally the Children's Centre environment was more conducive to messy play experiences than Josie's flat because it was specifically designed with children's play in mind. Providing such an experience in her home environment needed to be managed sensitively and the reasons for suggesting it had to be explained clearly, confidently and with reassurance.

The play opportunity could not happen unless Josie trusted the judgement of the practitioner. From experiences in Family Time, Josie was now not worried about any mess. She knew she could plan to deal with such practicalities. However, safety issues were discussed at length and strategies worked through so that the play was manageable for her and safe enough for the children so that baby Ben could also be involved. Working in this way fulfilled the requirement of the EYFS to provide a 'secure and safe environment' in which to play (DCSF, 2008c). In order for play to be sustained the activity had to be adapted to fit the family and environment in a realistic manner. Practitioners needed to be prepared to model the activity at home and reflect on what it might be like to be this particular mother providing this play and meeting Charlotte's demands for attention, whilst also enabling Ben to be part of the experience. Subsequently, Josie felt happy to have shallow water in a washing up bowl on the kitchen floor. She provided cups, small jugs and plastic bottles with a water wheel and an air pump operated shower borrowed from the outreach team's resources. Josie also produced items from her own cupboard, which might not have previously been introduced for play. This reflected her observation of the resources at Family Time and her knowledge that Charlotte enjoyed using all of these. The EYFS acknowledges that free play explorations are the foundation on which further learning takes place and this was a practical example of how this can happen.

In the following weeks Josie felt confident enough to use the local paddling pool at the park and took great pride in photographing the children having fun. Whilst Charlotte's drinking skills were still developing, the fact that water play was being carried out between visits was indicative of the success of modelling play and the discussions around it. The links between drinking skills and water play were difficult for Josie to comprehend and were not a primary motivating factor for providing water play, but having witnessed the children's happiness during supported play Josie was motivated to make her own play provision independently. She too was gaining some control over her circumstances. The photographs that Josie showed the home visitor revealed a happy family at play and that was the most important outcome of all because through play, language, emotional, physical and social skills are supported and these achievements sit comfortably within the EYFS.

Josie was enthused by her ability to provide some valuable play for the children and asked about gloop (a mixture of cornflour and water) that had excited her eldest child, Josh, so much. Gloop has interesting properties for children to explore and Josie observed Josh becoming immersed in touching, handling, stroking and squeezing this. His concentration was maintained for lengthy periods of time and Josie felt he was really calm during this play. This could have been due to the fact that there was no right or wrong way to play with gloop, there was no end product but the experience was very worthwhile. Indeed, being able to concentrate provided Josh with a greater ability to be able to pay attention and focus. Josh benefitted from such a play process as he strove to make sense of the new circumstances at home and the lack of contact with his father. The outreach worker encouraged Josie to provide positive support and encouragement for this play with Charlotte and Josh, as it would improve their ability to sustain play together and was vital to supporting a sense of emotional wellbeing between them. This, in turn influenced motivation, curiosity and a willingness to explore and also the resilience to be able to deal with life experiences.

Non-directive play opportunities such as gloop and heuristic play can cross national and cultural boundaries because they focus on children's exploration, curiosity and creativity in using materials in open-ended ways. This approach to play demonstrates regular social exchanges in child/child interactions and child/adult interactions. The play resources generate sociable communication and behaviour as children enjoy sensory stimulation through exploring natural and everyday materials. What is crucial to practitioners working with families in the home or setting is the recognition of these strengths, utilising them to their best advantage whilst building on sensorimotor and discovery play. Many of the resources used in heuristic play can also be combined with a provision of sensory play in environments for children with more complex needs. A focus on the sensory development of children with special needs can adapt to the needs of very young babies, encouraging basic skills such as grasping objects and visual eye tracking. Robinson (2008) also suggests that being conscious of oneself and the wider world begins with the care that a child receives from attentive adults and makes the point that being aware and able to think is a very sophisticated process that can be supported through early physical and sensory play. Josie and the practitioner both felt that heuristic play at home could also support the older children's acceptance of Ben if he were seen to 'participate' in playing. For Josie's young children, heuristic play became a 'bridge' between their different abilities and established moments of calm in a busy routine. Charlotte learnt to share her play space, play time and play materials with her little brother even if he could not quite be her playmate. Sensory play gradually took precedence in the family and Josie noticed that these opportunities sustained the children's involvement more than play with bought objects.

As a result of the relationship between Josie and the visiting practitioner, Josie's home became a significant part of the environment in which the interchange between adults and 'settings' actively promoted the development potential of the children. Ben was very young but was nevertheless learning to play and communicate. The practitioner also started to establish a relationship with him – a sensitive process as she was aware of not undermining Josie's confidence in her parenting decisions. Interaction with Ben started at the point of establishing eye contact and recognition and gradually built up to more sophisticated interactions but always by using Josie's lead. Enabling Josie to recognise the way she could use her home as a stimulating environment for play also involved thinking about reducing other distractions for the children, such as turning off the television. Visualising the living space as a play space might have meant that Josie needed to re-arrange furniture, or put away other items of the children's toys, especially when she was thinking about heuristic play. In particularly quiet times when Charlotte may have been having a nap, Josie could use some of the toy library equipment to provide music or sing to Ben as modelled in the Bumps and Babes play session. The relationship between the adults was ongoing, but as a result of play connections a continuity in positive experiences was established for the children in the wider environment.

Continuing Professional Development Activity

In the case study Josie's story represents a long journey of personal experience and building positive relationship with practitioners. In this CPD activity you will have the opportunity to reflect on your role and how you can support the needs of the child, the parent, the setting, and potentially other professionals.

Reflecting on your positive relationships in play

Aim

- To reflect on how you build positive relationships through play to support the needs of the child.

- To consider how you can focus on play to involve parents in your setting to make better or new connections.

- To explore the connections that you make with other professionals and the value this brings to supporting both the individual child and groups of children.

 Activity

Part 1

1 As an individual or with colleagues note down some of the ways in which your provision opens up a dialogue between parents and practitioners in identifying the needs of the child in the setting. For example, do you meet on a regular basis as a group, such as holding a parents' evening, or have a one-to-one discussion when a parent collects their child? Do you have communication books that can travel between home and the setting?

2 Think about how often you discuss aspects of play with parents. Is this the main focus when you communicate? Do they understand the ethos of your setting and where play fits in to that? Focus on your induction process when new children join your setting and consider how play is introduced and explained to parents.

3 After you have discussed points 1 and 2 split into pairs and engage in a role play where one of you takes the role of a parent and the other the practitioner. Here the practitioner must explain to the parent how play is used to build positive relationships between the child, practitioners, and parents. Ask for your partner's view on how you were able to articulate and reflect the reality of your setting.

Part 2

1 Identify the links and networks you are actively engaged in with 'outside' professionals if you are not part of a centre-based team. You may want to represent this as a diagram or flow chart.

2 Within usual practice the Common Assessment Framework (CAF) may well have been initiated to support Josie's children in the case study – discuss with your colleagues how you have organised your provision for engaging in this process and whether it has been a valuable tool in supporting connections between home, the setting, and other professionals.

3 Now look back at the development of the case study and highlight any action taken by the practitioner which:

- built on Josie's strengths and empowered her as a parent;
- applied specific theory to day-to-day practice;
- promoted child-centred play at all times.

Questions to consider

- *Why should play be central to the connections made between home, the setting, and key workers?*

Most adults can recall a memory about playing from their childhood and therefore it is a good starting point in opening up a dialogue to find out about a child's likes and dislikes, their family situation, and the level of engagement parents have with their children. Play should not make a judgement about achievement or skill so parents should feel able to contribute to a conversation which is based on what their child enjoys doing. Knowing this can help you as a practitioner to learn about a child's interests, which types of play a child already feels confident with, and where they may need support. The conversation about play with parents should always start from a 'can do' perspective and often involve the retelling of a scenario or game. This will mean that the parent can feel involved and may often offer similar examples of behaviours re-enacted at home. Consequently the practitioner can receive information about the child's family life and can offer further play opportunities to the child or support to the family.

- *What are you going to do to make more meaningful connections with parents?*

Your setting may be very different from the Children's Centre presented in the case study, yet issues in supporting parents to meet the play needs of children are universal. Your reflection on the CPD activity and the case study are important in terms of your values relating to play-based practice. If you are able to centre your discussions on the child's play and approach future support and learning from a play-centred perspective, you can reflect the significance of play back to the parent. This will help them to engage and communicate with you in a more play-focused way. You may need to develop strategies to support parents in thinking about the value of play and the example in the case study involving water play to support drinking co-ordination is a good one here. You will need to examine your practice in terms of putting play at the centre of what you do in order to support parents to think about their play interactions with their children.

- *How will you convince other professionals that play is important?*

Each professional with whom you have contact will have their own agenda for supporting an individual child. It is important that you become an advocate for play within that process, so for example a child with a speech delay can receive specialist help delivered in a playful context which will stimulate that child's interests. Observations and assessments can be made without resorting to a 'worksheet' mentality but this may require you to model to other professionals ways in which a child can be an active participant through play. Your perspective represents the voice of the child, so if play is taken out of the situation because it is deemed unnecessary you then move away from a child-centred approach towards an outcome-led agenda.

Summary

This chapter has examined the connections made between home, the setting and practitioners in response to the case study and the guidance given in the EYFS. It has highlighted the importance of understanding and responding sensitively to the experiences and needs of the family in making meaningful connections. Building up a picture of the family unit, the wider community, and how they 'fit' with your setting has also been a central theme of this chapter. It has examined the role of working together and using play to support the voice of the child and the development needs of the family. In practice supporting the connections between parents and the setting is an ongoing and ever evolving relationship. Your skills in negotiation between the child's need to engage in valuable play, parents' wishes, and the principles of practice rely on your ability to advocate play and facilitate 'play connections.'

Section 3

Enabling Environments

'Enabling environments explain that the environment plays a key role in supporting and extending children's development and learning. The commitments are focused around observation, assessment and planning; support for every child, the learning environment and the wider context – transitions, continuity and multi-agency working.' (DCSF, 2008f: 9)

Enabling Environments

 Case Study: Using Indoor and Outdoor Spaces

Natalie Canning

The children in this case study are aged between three and four years old. It is based on a non-participant narrative observation of play in a private rural day nursery.

Jack, Marcus and William attend a private full-day care nursery. The nursery benefits from a large outdoor play space which has a grass area, several mature trees, a winding path around the main building, a shed containing outdoor toys, tricycles and bikes, and raised flower and vegetable patches in one corner. The outdoor space is mainly flat and the nursery operates a free flow play policy where possible to ensure maximum use of the space. Leading out from the nursery doors is a canopy with a patio area so that inside activities can be taken outside, and to enable free flow play, even when the weather is changeable. The nursery is organised so that just inside the door to the outdoor space, craft and messy activities can take place and often these will spill out to the patio and covered area. The nursery has extensive planning where all members of staff are included. Spreadsheets are colour co-ordinated according to the four principles and six areas of learning in the EYFS and each child has a book containing their learning journey. The daily routine is organised around a series of free play opportunities and more structured playful activities that build on their interests and explorations, where children are encouraged and expected to take part.

Jack, Marcus and William are engaged in a free play opportunity where they have gravitated towards the construction area of the nursery and are building a tower out of wooden blocks. They are best friends and spend most of their time together when they are at nursery. They have been building the tower as high as they can before it collapses, but they soon tire of the game and decide to go outside and play football on the grass. They kick the ball between them for a short time and then William says 'We could kick the ball high, higher than a tower, up to the sky!' Jack and Marcus like this idea and the boys start to take it in turns to try and kick the ball into the air. Predictably the ball doesn't go up but along the ground, hitting the boundary fence. Marcus stops and says, 'It needs to go up, not over there', Jack goes to retrieve the ball, carries it back and then throws it in the air. 'Up to the sky!' he shouts and jumps up and down on the spot clapping his hands. When the ball lands he retrieves it and the other two take it in turns to throw the ball in the air. As they do this, they move away from the grassy area towards a tree. William throws the ball into the air and it lodges in its lower branches. It's too high for the boys to reach it and they enter into a detailed discussion on how they are going to retrieve the ball. They suggest shaking the tree, climbing it, getting something to knock the ball, standing on top of each other to reach it, and they even try out some of these ideas to see if any will work. Eventually they ask Sarah, the practitioner, to help. She has been quietly watching the boys to make sure they were safe, but has not interrupted their play or problem solving.

The setting encourages children to explore the outdoor space as much as possible. Several of the staff have attended forest school training and the setting has negotiated with the farm next door to use a small wooded area to build dens and set up a 'camp' with space for an open fire in a small clearing. Sarah has seen the improvement in Jack since he has been attending sessions in the forest school. His parents have recently separated and except when he is with Marcus and William, Jack spends a lot of time by himself. When he goes to the forest school he seems to relax and really enjoys building dens and finding wood for the fire. Sarah has noticed that he becomes more confident and shows clear communication skills, telling the other children how to build dens. Sarah is discussing with her team how they can support Jack through this transition period and is considering how she can utilise the environment to do this.

Exploring the Possibilities of the Play Environment

Natalie Canning

Chapter Objectives

This chapter demonstrates how the environment plays a fundamental part in supporting the play experiences of children and how experience supports children's exploration, confidence, and personal development. It explores the challenge of providing play environments which meet the needs of all children, within the setting's parameters and using resources available. The importance of risky play opportunities is examined and the chapter argues that children need to experience an environment which facilitates risk in some way. It examines some of the complexities in planning for play and stresses the importance of practitioners' shared understanding and knowledge about play environments and the processes of play which exist within them.

The play experience

Children's play is influenced by their environment. It both accommodates and limits what children want to do in their play and when they want to do it. Many of the skills children develop and master are based on the environment in which they are able to explore, take risks, and do things for themselves. Mooney (2000) emphasises that children should be active and interactive in their environments and

93

that this will support learning opportunities. The EYFS also emphasises this by stating that there should be 'time and space for children
to concentrate on activities and experiences and to develop their
own interests' (DCSF, 2008e: 23). Consequently, how play environments are perceived by practitioners directly impacts on the play
experiences of children. Greene and Hill (2005) suggest that how we
relate to the world is largely a function of the cultural context of our
society. This is very apparent when considering the play experience
of children in different countries. Practitioners who have considered
implementing the Scandinavian model of outdoor play in the UK
have supported the philosophy but also discovered that the perception of play, the significance placed upon risk and danger and the
way in which policy and practice is driven by achieving formal outcomes make it very difficult to implement.

The play experiences offered to children by practitioners reflect a
socially constructed view of childhood (Waller, 2005). Practitioners'
view of what constitutes positive experiences within a play environment originates largely from their experiences; an adult construction
of what they think children will find stimulating and enjoy. Mayall
(2002) argues that childhood is an adult construction and is
informed by the culture of the surrounding community. This is true
in the case study, as the setting's environment reflects a local rural
community with importance being placed on the outdoors, reflecting the farming backgrounds of many of the families. However, the
practitioners in the setting also realise that childhood is not static or
a universal experience for all children and therefore try hard to provide different opportunities via the facilities they have within their
indoor and outdoor environment. Walkerdine (2004) identifies that
childhood is mobile and shifting, something that is recognised by
the practitioners in the case study as they work towards 'creating a
stimulating environment that offers a range of activities, encouraging children's interest and curiosity' (DCSF, 2008e: 75). Sarah, the
practitioner in the case study, commented:

> We have really tried hard as a setting to utilise the environment to provide an
> inclusive space for all children. We sometimes take it for granted that we have
> such a resourceful outdoor space and recently we have had some new children
> start who have just moved to the area. They have come from a large city, so to
> suddenly be faced with such a large outdoor area was really daunting for them.
> They initially found it hard to engage with more physical play and as a team
> we had to think carefully about how to support them in the environment. It
> highlighted to us that we take our way of life for granted and that children's
> experiences are not all the same. (Interview, July 2009)

This view underpins the way in which meeting individual children's
needs, even in a well-resourced setting, can provide a challenge for prac-

titioners. Sarah commented that she saw her primary role as supporting children's confidence to undertake risks and challenge, scaffolding them to use all of the opportunities the play space offered. The setting in the case study found that by simply changing the position of play equipment, it became more dynamic and flexible for the children to use. Kadis (2007) argues that for a play space to be effective it needs to provide interest and give children sufficient choice and flexibility so that they keep revisiting and exploring different ways to use the materials. Sarah found that using heuristic play with children before they experienced a forest school environment for the first time gave younger children the confidence to explore their environment and experiment with materials. In heuristic play young children are encouraged to use materials in a process of trial and error rather than playing to set rules or a specified outcome. In the case study this mirrored the setting's philosophy towards the forest school where experiencing the natural world through practical involvement and exploration was encouraged. In both heuristic and forest school play children are able to demonstrate their preferences and start to build relationships through social and communication play. Heuristic play naturally reflects children's cultural influences and unique qualities, providing practitioners with insights into their likes and dislikes. An environment which stimulates and enables children to make choices, explore, and satisfy their curiosity gives them new experiences and challenges to develop new skills. This not only provides a foundation for children's learning and development, but also an opportunity for practitioners to observe the choices that children make and reflect on how their home and setting can influence what they say and do (Goldschmied and Jackson, 2004).

The case study illustrates the way that the three boys are confident playing within the boundaries of the inside and outside space. They are familiar with their environment and confident in expressing themselves. As a practitioner Sarah has always felt that developing children's awareness of difference and diversity should be much more than posters on the wall highlighting different languages and images of children, but without knowledge and a first-hand experience of different cultures she felt ill equipped to know how to improve this in her day-to-day practice without paying 'lip service' to equality, diversity, and difference. The EYFS statement 'You must promote positive attitudes to diversity and difference within all children. In doing this you will help them to learn to value different aspects of their own and other people's lives' (DCSF, 2008e: 6) hadn't helped Sarah to resolve her anxiety in providing different play opportunities which reflect difference and diversity. The sweeping statement from the EYFS doesn't provide enough detail on what this looks like in practice. With her team Sarah discussed the idea of difference, diversity and cultural expectations and how they could find ways to make this accessible and meaningful in their practice. At the same time they were engaging in a discussion about risk taking in the forest school environment and Sarah reflected that it was interesting to hear other practitioner views on the subject. This made her think about how the evolving culture of the setting could be linked to the attitude towards risk taking.

Previously Sarah had not considered the impact of small changes, for example, encouraging children to take risks and how these could influence the culture of the setting in a small way which could then lead to tackling some of the bigger issues. McNaughton (2003) emphasises that a child's development is a cultural construction based on our cultural understandings and biases of what we do, how we do it, and what it means to us. This perspective is important when considering the EYFS statements. For example, 'provide a stimulating environment in which creativity, originality and expressiveness are valued' (DCSF, 2008e: 105) will be translated into practice in different ways depending on practitioners' socially constructed view of culture. This may restrict children's experiences of play because it does not 'fit' with the expectations of the setting, parents, or the wider community. This argument is the starting point for thinking about how to develop risk taking in play.

Risky play

The Department of Health (DoH, 2004) offers a view that taking risks, experimenting, and pushing boundaries are each an important part of growing up. Children need opportunities to learn about their world in ways that can provide challenge and excitement through positive things to do and opportunities to play. Stephenson (2003) conducted a study in New Zealand that revealed risk for four year olds consisted of:

- attempting something not done before;

- being on the edge of out of control;

- overcoming fear.

The risk often included swinging, sliding and climbing. As early years professionals the arguments to provide risk taking opportunities for children are compelling. Ludvigsen et al. (2005) contend that if play is too safe, it limits children's practical experiences of risk management and may affect their ability to recognise and deal with risky situations. Risk in play supports children to explore their limits and develop their capacities from an early age. Children will often have a 'risk monitor' within them, knowing how far they want to go with the risk – for example, how high they want to jump or climb. If children are not able to test this risk monitor they do not learn how to self regulate what they are feeling or overcome fear. Play is an ideal situation where children can test this out. In a setting a safe environment is provided, with qualified and skilled professionals to support children's development. It offers a situation where children can experience acceptable risk as part of stimulating and challenging play.

These are important driving forces for 'risky play', however the resisting forces are perhaps a fear of litigation if things go wrong or a child is hurt. The result may be that protecting children from risk goes too far. If they are not allowed to build towers from wooden blocks higher than their waist or walk over the rocks at the seaside on an outing, then children cannot build the capacity to master skills or conquer their fears. The EYFS states that 'through play, in a secure but challenging environment with effective adult support children can take risks and make mistakes' (DCSF, 2008e: 8). In the physical development section of areas of learning it also states that practitioners should 'ensure children's safety, while not unduly inhibiting their risk-taking' (DCSF, 2008e: 100). Throughout the practice guidance heavy emphasis is placed on the need for safety, risk assessments, and the ability to 'reappraise the environments and activities to which children are being exposed to and make necessary adjustments to secure their safety at all times' (DCSF, 2008e: 20). Safety should not be compromised over risk taking, but professionally evaluated risks are necessary for children to experience and learn. The Play Safety Forum which sits within Play England suggests that an informed understanding of the balance between risk and benefit is based on three factors:

- the likelihood of coming to harm;

- the severity of that harm;

- the benefits, rewards, or outcomes of the activity (Sutcliffe, 2007: 9).

These indicators can help determine whether the level of risk is acceptable to the setting. The summary statement from the Play Safety Forum states that:

> Children need and want to take risks when they play. Play provision aims to respond to these needs and wishes by offering children stimulating, challenging environments for exploring and developing their abilities. In doing this, play provision aims to manage the level of risk so that children are not exposed to unacceptable risks of death or serious injury. (Play England, 2008: 1)

Sutcliffe (2007) reports that this statement has helped many settings to assess risk taking within their setting and has been used as a starting point for balancing the importance of risk in play, the positive opportunities it can create, the fear factor amongst adults, and a rational approach to planning for risk in play. The Children's Plan (DCSF, 2007c: 5) attempts to address the issue of balancing risk and safety, establishing as one of its five principles that 'children need to enjoy their childhood as well as grow up prepared for adult life'. Risk taking is a part of everyday life and therefore to ensure that children are prepared for the future, they need to start to take risks at a young age.

Planning through the environment

The play environment is a central resource to provide rich opportunities to help planning to support free play and more structured play opportunities. It underlines the ethos of a setting and tells parents and carers about the collective view of risk, care for others and the environment, choice, and the way the physical space and resources are intended to stimulate and motivate children. In using the environment it is important to assess what it already offers in terms of:

- expanding what children already know;

- supporting children to develop their skills;

- facilitating children's understanding about the world around them;

- developing their creativity;

- supporting their problem-solving skills;

- providing opportunities for social engagement;

- supporting physical skills such as fine and gross motor development.

By doing this you are ensuring that planning skills are located in your daily practice and are naturally occurring. This goes some way to enabling 'spontaneous play' to occur (DCSF, 2008e: 7). If the environment stimulates and inspires children's imaginations they can provide you as the practitioner with rich material on which you can base your planning and think about appropriate resources for your setting. In the case study the transition between the block play indoors and the ball game outside may initially have seemed unrelated. However, the content of the boys' play reflected an up and down schema that they had been engaged in for a few weeks. The repetition of building a tall tower with the wood bricks and subsequently knocking it down, the attempts at throwing the ball in the air and watching it come down, and the physical movement of handling the ball in the motion of bending low and jumping high with arms stretched upwards all indicated to Sarah, the practitioner, that the boys were motivated to include this schema in their play. She reflected on how this would impact on her planning for their individual learning journeys:

> I think that recognising the way in which Jack in particular uses an up and down schema in his play will really help me to think about how I can provide further opportunities for him to practise his skills. I know he feels really at home in the forest school so I'm going to suggest that we move some logs into more accessible places so that the children can climb on them and jump off. I know he would love that. It would also be great to identify a few trees which could be suitable for climbing, not too high, but I know there is a smallish one, where we could encourage the children to take risks. (Interview, July 2009)

Sarah's thinking and subsequent planning was play based in that climbing the logs was not something that the children had to do as part of an activity, but by making them available in the play environment, Sarah had a good feeling from her previous observations of Jack that he would engage in physical play using an up and down schema. She therefore extended his play experience by recognising his interests, identifying where he felt confident, and providing resources that would support his development. Of course Jack may not have chosen to take the opportunity Sarah envisaged, but may also reveal other interests through playing with the logs in different ways or even ignoring them completely. A couple of weeks later Sarah reflected:

> Jack did use the logs in the way I had predicted and we were able to extend this further by supervising him to climb a small tree. He was so excited! I had to persuade my colleagues that this would be a good thing and remind them that forest school, and all play really, is about building on children's motivation and positive attitudes towards doing new things. I want to be the one who offers them new opportunities to take risks, make choices, and see them grow as individuals, and it's so rewarding to see Jack smile and have a sense of achievement when I know things are not so good at home. It was worth the form filling for the risk assessment and the discussions I had with some colleagues and parents who weren't so keen on the idea. (Interview, August 2009)

Sarah had taken into consideration not only Jack's interests when she was planning for further play opportunities, but also the way in which she could use the environment to encourage him to continue his up and down schema without planning specifically for this to happen. She provided the possibility for him to take a play decision that was based on what she knew about the children in her care and the resources she could utilise within the environment. Through applying this approach in her practice she ensured that there was 'planning for the group while keeping a focus on children's individual and present learning needs or interests and achievements' (DCSF, 2008b). Sarah continued:

> I didn't just plan for Jack, but made sure that the forest school environment provided opportunities for other children to explore and take small risks. Some of the children sat on the logs whilst others ran around them. Some children didn't want to climb the tree but I tried to make sure that the play space allowed for all the children to take part and have a choice in what they wanted to do. It was good because I could follow the child's lead and wasn't restricted by what was or wasn't in the play space. (Interview, August 2009)

Brown (2003) introduces the idea that by having a flexible environment, you create a flexible child who can adapt and be resourceful in other situations. He argues that when an environment has flexible potential, it facilitates a child's potential for curiosity, problem solving, and creativity. He identifies this as 'compound flexibility' and suggests that it 'is the interrelationship between a flexible/adaptable environment and the gradual development of flexibility/adaptability in the child' (2003: 53). The environment is then proactive in enabling the practitioner to stay centred on the children and has the capacity to enable the child to evolve their play. In a flexible environment, the practitioner also has to be aware of the way in which the child may use the materials and potentially how they may also misuse them. Sarah reflected:

> We have some children that can get over excited when we go to forest school. We allow a certain amount of rough and tumble and physical play outside, especially for the boys, but we have to watch that it doesn't get out of hand, or that too many children become involved. I guess the downside of a flexible environment is that sometimes the children become too confident in the play space and then it's our job to see it before it happens and direct the children to another focus. It started to get a bit like this with Jack and his friends. They became confident and excited when they had climbed and jumped off the log a few times. Jane and I then directed them to the tree – much more of a challenge! You could see that they were apprehensive but we supported them and built on their courage and success of managing the log. (Interview, August 2009)

Sarah's experience highlights that the way in which play develops is not only dependent upon the environment but also on the sensitivity of the practitioner. The environment can influence play, but so can the relationship you have with the children in the play space. This returns to two of the core themes of this book – establishing a trusting relationship with children and maintaining a balance in supporting children's development whilst allowing them opportunities for free play, a spontaneous exploration of ideas, and a nurturing of their curiosity and risk taking.

Continuing Professional Development Activity

In order for children to take risks it is important to explore if you are a risk taker. This will influence how you plan for risky play in your setting and also how you work with children and colleagues to provide new play opportunities. Understanding what constitutes risk for children has implications for practitioners as the risk needs to be incorporated into a natural progression of the play children want to engage with and how the environment can support it. There is no point in planning risk in play if it is completely unrelated to children's interests.

When did you last take a risk?

Aims

- To explore if you are a risk taker.

- To examine how this impacts on how you plan and provide for risky play.

- To consider your setting's position on risk taking.

 Activity

Part 1 – Your approach to taking risks

1 Think back to the last time you took a risk. This can be anything in your personal or professional life. It could be a small risk, with minimal consequences – for example, trying out a new recipe on friends and family – or something bigger, such as moving house or changing your job.

2 When you have thought of an example reflect on the following:

- At the time did you identify the decision as taking a risk or as something else?

- Did you make the decision to take the risk on your own or with others?

- How did you feel before you finalised your decision to take the risk?

- How did you feel when you were involved in the risk?

- What were the consequences of taking the risk?

- What were the benefits or drawbacks of taking the risk?

- How has taking the risk influenced your confidence in taking further risks?

3 In the next week keep a record of how many times you take risks during your day-to-day and work activity. What constitutes a risk is down

to you – for example, some people might consider driving to work a risk whilst others may not. The tally at the end of the week and the type of risks you have recorded will indicate how much of a risk taker you are.

4 Share your results with colleagues and compare your tally with theirs and what constituted a risk for you. Do you have different views? Discuss your approach to risk taking and the feelings that taking risks provokes.

Part 2 – Taking risks with children

5 Now consider how your views on risk taking translate into your work with children. Reflect on whether you feel the same about allowing children to take risks as you feel about taking risks yourself.

- What might be the different elements you have to consider when supporting children taking risks?

- Do you think that you provide children with opportunities to take risks in your planning? Think of an example and share this with your colleagues. Do they have similar experiences?

6 In the case study Sarah extended Jack's play by recognising an up and down schema he was involved in and incorporating opportunities for him to extend this through small risk taking steps (climbing the logs). This prepared Jack for bigger risk-taking opportunities which required more structured support from Sarah (climbing the tree). Can you identify a similar example from your practice where you have planned and supported children to take risks in their environment?

7 Complete the table below to help you structure your thoughts.

Table 7.1 Taking risks with children

Outline of the original planned play	Elements of the play you identified where you could extend children's experiences	Risk taking that could be incorporated into the play	Predicted or actual reactions by the children to your plans to challenge their play	Potential learning for the children involved in the play

8 Use the table as a starting point to structure a team discussion to plan for risk taking in your setting. If you base your planning on an adaptable and open play space then you will have greater flexibility to respond to children's needs.

9 Experiment by placing restrictions on your play resources and space and observe the reactions you get from children's play behaviour. From your observations what impact will this have on your approach to risk in play?

Questions to consider

• *What are the benefits and challenges of providing risky play opportunities in your setting?*

This question is something that you will need to assess alongside your colleagues. Often it is not the fact that you cannot reach a consensus about what is valuable for children to do in your setting in terms of play, learning and development, but how to approach it and implement it that can raise interesting debates. If you want to support greater opportunities for risky play then the Play England website provides constructive and practical guidance for settings. It is also important to ensure that the child is at the centre of the process in developing risky play. Observe what they do in a free play situation and then consider if any of it involves taking risks – how far are they trying to push the boundaries of the play space and the setting's resources?

• *In the case study Sarah saw the benefit of providing flexible play environments to facilitate inclusion for children in her setting. Can you identify examples of how this might support your practice?*

The EYFS guidance on supporting inclusion, diversity, equality, and cultural differences provides sweeping statements based on achieving outcomes for children. The detail and process of what happens in the setting are overlooked in the guidance and are left to the setting to decide on in how to approach and implement these essential elements of practice. In the case study example Sarah, the practitioner, found that by reflecting on how she planned for risk taking in play she was able to recognise how she contributed to change in her setting. Through exploring different approaches to risky play in the forest school she was able to introduce a small shift in thinking and therefore in the overall approach of the setting towards taking risks in play. Her actions allowed others to see how she had incorporated risk into her planning for play and therefore supported children in gaining new experiences, trying out different play, and supporting all the children in the setting to try something different. Sarah was supported by a flexible environment which allowed her to give children the opportunity to experience new skills, but also resources that could be utilised in different ways without fixed uses or prescribed outcomes. The resources relied on Sarah using them in a creative and child-centred way to facilitate schema development and meaningful play experiences.

- *In the case study the forest school provided Sarah with a platform for planning acceptable risk taking for Jack and his friends. How might your environment support you in planning for greater free play opportunities?*

The environment is your greatest asset in supporting your setting's vision and ethos for play. It reflects what you value and how you approach children's development. Take a moment to assess your setting's environment – what does it tell you about how you support child-centred play? Does it reflect a particular philosophy or approach, such as Steiner who advocated natural resources, or Reggio Emila who stressed the importance of a central meeting place – the 'plaza' (Malauzzi, 1994). Or does it reflect influence from more than one Early Childhood pioneer? In evaluating your environment you may gain an insight into how you could rearrange or change your physical space to reflect the ethos you want to create for play. Question whether you provide flexibility in your resources for children to explore their creativity and imagination. How do you support different types of play to occur naturally? Assessing your play space in this way may help you to think about how you plan for play and how your environment can support you in observing and assessing play that children engage with without resorting to prescribed play activities.

Summary

This chapter has explored how the environment is fundamental to the play experience of children and how their confidence and personal development can be supported by a flexible and adaptable space. It has examined the challenge of providing risky play experiences and has also questioned the implications for practice from the EYFS guidance. Using the environment in planning for play has been a central theme alongside the importance of a shared understanding and knowledge held by practitioners about play environments and the processes of play which occur within them. It has reflected on Sarah's experience of utilising the environment to provide meaningful and fulfilling play opportunities for Jack and his friends. It has also demonstrated how recognising the child's interests, in this case through developing schemas, can provide rich ideas for planning and developing children's skills, learning, and development.

Play Environments in Practice

Natalie Canning

Chapter Objectives

This chapter places the child at the centre of the play environment and considers the opportunities that practitioners can provide for children to challenge themselves through play. It examines the impact of the environment in supporting challenging experiences and assesses the balance between outdoor and indoor play environments. It also considers what quality play may look like and how practitioners can facilitate quality within the systems, policies and procedures that operate within settings.

Challenging play

In the previous chapter providing risk-taking opportunities through play was explored. Risk and challenge are interconnected as children try something new and push their own boundaries to develop a skill. In the case study Marcus had been learning to ride his bike. He started with stabilisers but recently reached the point where he was ready for them to be removed. His parents usually brought the bike with them to collect Marcus from the day nursery and he practised riding his bike home every day. At the first attempt without stabilisers he was nervous and wobbly and lost his balance several times, causing him frustration. However, after practising the skill and rising to the challenge he was able to cycle by himself. A number of factors contributed to his eventual success:

- Marcus made the decision that he wanted to ride his bike without stabilisers – he was motivated and determined;

- he experimented with his balance and coordination, learning from his mistakes;

- he practised the skill of riding the bike and this built up his confidence;

- he experienced a sense of achievement each time he attempted to ride the bike and managed to go a bit further before falling off;

- deciding to ride the bike created a moment of anticipation at the end of each day and a rush of adrenalin as he attempted to cycle.

Kadis (2007) states that these are essential elements for children, so that they push their own boundaries and revisit challenging situations to explore other ways of doing things. Although learning to ride a bike could be viewed as an activity with an end goal rather than play, it was interesting to see that Marcus played within the process of working towards what he wanted to achieve. For example, the environment was a crucial element in his decision where to mount the bike and where to have his first attempt at riding by himself. He chose a grassy area which was fairly flat and he inspected the ground before having a go. When asked what he was doing he said 'checking for bumps', demonstrating his regard for self-preservation, his problem-solving ability and his creativity in thinking about this in the first place! Kadis argues that children need to keep revisiting challenge as it supports them in exploring solutions and making decisions based on their experiences as well as helping them to think strategically about how to achieve their aim. For a play space to be effective within a setting it has to hold an element of risk to help children evaluate their capabilities and judge situations. Kadis argues that as long as the risk is managed by making it obvious to children where the dangers lie, and practitioners ensure that the equipment isn't hazardous, then a balance can be created.

There are challenges for children in play at many different levels. In the case study Marcus, Jack and William were good friends but another boy, Adam, who is quite shy but would like to join in with their games, would often stand on the periphery of their play, hoping to be asked or accepted into it. Sarah, the practitioner, noted:

Adam wants to be accepted into the play but he has to challenge himself to ask to join in and risk being rejected by the others. He has tried several strategies to let the boys know he is there, engaging in parallel play and trying to join in conversation about what they are doing or building. So far it hasn't quite worked, but he is building up his confidence and I think the forest school will be the perfect place to support him in integrating with those boys. (Interview, August 2009)

Sarah was quietly encouraging of Adam without intervening in his attempts to make friends. She was aware that it was his personal challenge and was allowing him the time and space to develop his own self-assurance. She commented:

If I make the introductions for him, he won't feel the same sense of achieve-ment, but that doesn't mean I'm not sensitive to his desire to join in and will facilitate this through the environment of the forest school and outdoor space as it is more flexible for him to join in and drift out of different types of play. (Interview, August 2009)

The EYFS states that 'a high quality continuously improving setting will provide ... challenging and appropriate play based content reflecting individual needs so that ... children develop relationships at all levels' (DCSF, 2008e: 8). Sarah was using the environment to help her not only to support children in undertaking risk and chal-lenge, but also to develop quality experiences so that they could develop their own skills in forming positive relationships with other children. At that moment Adam may have felt anxious about mak-ing connections with the other boys, but it was his personal challenge to build friendships, supported by an enabling environ-ment and sensitive key workers.

Quality play

Consequently it is important for practitioners to think about the quality of play that children engage in and the quality of the experiences provided. Children may be involved in a whole range of play such as imaginative play when pretending to be a police officer, but it is not enough just to recognise the play and label it: it is important to consider the implications of the play for each child. This is also true of the six areas of learning and 'development matters' section of the EYFS. In observing and assessing children's play it is not enough for the skill simply to be recognised, it is necessary to know the quality of the interaction, what the child is gaining from the play, and how it can be extended. When a greater depth of thinking is applied to what children do and how they do this in play, it becomes more than a 'tick list' of achievements and starts to have real meaning from a holistic view of development.

However, this subsequently relies on two further factors – the quality of the play environment and the ability of the practitioner in facilitating play in a flexible way to afford children the best opportunity to explore their surroundings. This means that the setting needs to have a structure where children know the boundaries and can play freely within them. It is also important to recognise within the structure of a typical day that there is an equal balance between free play (where children have choice and autonomy about what they play with and where they play) and activities led by practitioners. The danger is that everything becomes defined as 'play' and thus it is more difficult to describe the purpose and focus for your practice. In thinking about recognising what quality play is, it is important to distinguish different practices which support children in different ways. Your setting's environment may be organised in such a way that facilitates certain types of play better than others. A practitioner's skill lies in recognising the way in which the environment is used and analysing how children utilise the space when given free choice. Alongside this practitioners need to identify what is appropriate and safe, to reflect on children's reactions based on the influence of the environment and use these skills to plan for future play opportunities which can build challenge, interest and skill.

Jackson (2010) conducted a study with practitioners to obtain their views on what they recognised as top priorities for quality. Planning for children's individual learning and development needs was closely followed by procedures and provision to support children with additional needs. This was in contrast to parents' views that placed children being well supervised at the top of their list. This highlights an interesting tension between expectations for practice. The different views of parents and practitioners suggest that the issue of quality play may not be high on the parental agenda and may also contribute to the struggle practitioners have in raising its status in their own settings. Quality indicators for play return to the debate that play is ambiguous (Sutton Smith, 1997) and therefore difficult to define. Sylva and Pugh (2005) suggest that as long as there are interpretative variations causing gaps and tension in what play looks like and means for practice this will lead to inconsistency in the delivery of a play-based curriculum for children. Consequently the National Strategies Early Years Quality Improvement Support Programme (EYQISP) (DCSF, 2008g) attempts to address this by providing tools for practitioners to use to raise quality within their setting. The tools are built on four key principles which are then explored through five elements and children's play is addressed via:

> supporting progress, learning and development, focusing on using observations to assess and understand children's learning and development ... translating observation of children at play into an assessment of each child's progress ... (DCSF, 2008g: 7)

This statement does not address quality in terms of the process where the child is at the centre of practice, but emphasises instead the outcome of assessment. In the same way the EYFS profile ensures that judgements are made in respect of 'children's progress towards the early learning goals' (DCSF, 2008e: 12). Consequently quality provision is seen as an outcome which practitioners feel obliged to work towards. In relation to the play environment this means that settings are often organised to meet the needs of practitioners in assessing children's progress rather than being spaces for play designed to provide the best possible play opportunities. To achieve a shift in focus requires careful thought and planning but this can be realised in the smallest or most ill-equipped setting. Shackell et al. (2008) suggest that one way in which to approach the design of your setting is to imagine you are a child and provide the sorts of spaces which you would appreciate – for example, hideaways and quiet spaces in balance with open areas for more physical play. These principles can be applied to both outdoor and indoor environments where the focus is placed on the design rather than resources. They advocate that well-designed spaces will outlive play resources because children will want to be part of the environment and to own and develop it. They will demonstrate their ability to play with minimal resources through imaginative and creative responses to what is available.

Play types

Therefore the flexibility of the resources you have and the way in which you use your play space will also go some way to supporting children who are exploring different types of play. Hughes (2002) outlined 15 different types of play in childhood. When children play they are usually engaged in at least one type of play, but these can be combined or start as one type and then move into another or a combination of types. For example, in the case study the boys were engaged in social play as they built a tower out of wooden blocks, they were each participating in constructing the tower, talking to each other about how they were going to build it, and responding to each other's suggestions. When they moved outside and played with the ball they were engaged in more physical and exploratory play as they kicked the ball, threw it up in the air, and attempted to dislodge it when it became stuck in the tree. The play revealed not only children's learning and understanding, but also a process of engagement, problem solving, and creativity from an unplanned play opportunity.

Some settings use types of play as a way in which to support observations of children because they provide an explanation of what the child is doing and a framework where practitioners can identify different areas of development. Critics would argue that play types are another way of categorising play and Wood and Attfield (2005: 7) argue that by labelling play 'we may be in danger of overlooking the fact that children define play themselves'. However, play types can provide a sense of structure for practitioners to recognise the engagement of children when they play and an alternative focus from 'development matters' in the EYFS if practitioners feel that their observations are becoming too concentrated on recording outcomes and missing the process of play.

Indoor *vs.* outdoor play

The EYFS states that 'children must have opportunities to play indoors and outdoors … all early years providers must have access to an outdoor play area which can benefit the children' (DCSF, 2008e: 7). It could be argued that any outside space would be of benefit to children as they can experience a different environment; however, the most successful indoor and outdoor experiences for children are when they have free flow opportunities (Bruce, 2005). Drawing from chaos theory as a model for play, Bruce argues that play generates spontaneous exploration and connections with others when it is in 'free flow'. Some of the characteristics of free flow play are that it:

- is an active process without a product;

- is intrinsically motivated;

- is about possible alternative worlds which involve 'supposing' and 'as if' and these encompass being imaginative, original, innovative, and creative;

- actively uses previous first-hand experiences, including struggle, manipulation, exploration, discovery, and practice;

- can be in partnership, or with groups of adults and/or children, who will be sensitive to each other;

- is an integrating mechanism, which brings together everything we learn, know, feel, and understand (Bruce, 2005).

In the case study, the boys decided when they would move from the indoor area to the outside space. They undertook different play in each of the areas, supported by a flexible environment where learning and development were seamlessly integrated into their play. Not every setting will have the space to support a large outdoor environment, but it is important that any outdoor space is not merely an extension of indoor resources. The outdoors provides rich opportunities for sensori-motor development, not only through natural materials such as leaves, grass, paving, or soil to name but a few, but also through the physicality of exploring the outside. True free-flow play is difficult to achieve for many settings and that is largely down to the staff ratio requirements. Children will explore their environment on their own terms which may mean they are inside and outside at the same time. Nevertheless it is important to consider ways in which outdoor play can be managed, so that even if free-flow play is not practically possible, a child's 'play diet' (Packard, 2006) can still include large elements of outdoor experiences. Packard states:

> If we are to really improve the quality of play opportunities we also need to provide children with access to more natural and creative play settings that help stimulate the senses and encourage greater use of the imagination. (cited in Shackell et al., 2008: 14)

Children's drive and desire to play are intrinsically motivated and is instinctive, but for optimum play to occur when children are deeply absorbed in what they are doing, the game they are playing or the fantasy they are creating is dependent upon access and the quality of play environments (Fjortoft, 2004). The organisation '11 million', led by the Children's Commissioner for England, asked children what was important in their play environments (11 million and Play England, 2008). They identified having choice and freedom in how they play, socialising with others, and having outdoor fun as vital to their play. Equally, the Good Childhood Inquiry (2009) – commissioned through The Children's Society – obtained over 18,000 views from children. They found that play featured as an important aspect of children's lives, with outside play being important. Children's main frustration was that there was not enough time or space to play and that play was usually restricted by an adult. They also placed importance on friendship, being listened to, and learning through doing (Layard and Dunn, 2009). Research where children's views are collected concludes that practitioners and settings, and particularly play environments, need to work towards reflecting the child's voice through careful planning and resourcing to meet their needs. Shackell et al. (2008: 15) also suggest that to achieve successful play spaces several factors need to be taken into account. These need to:

- offer movement and physical activity;

- stimulate the senses;

- provide opportunity for social interaction;

- provide an opportunity for challenge;

- manipulate natural and man-made materials.

In addition they point out that play can be about extremes and doing lots of things which do not always have clear connections: for example, moving between being social in play but also being alone and working through problems in their own way. To facilitate these aspects play environments need to have flexibility, not only as regards the physical space but also as part of the systems that ensure settings run smoothly.

Stuck in a rut?

Research by Dudek (2000) found that the boundaries a setting operates within are key to determining what type of values and ethos are sustained by practitioners, how this translates to children's involvement and ownership of the setting, and the way in which the setting contributes overall to building relationships between practitioners, children, and parents. Dudek (2000: 24) states that 'in order to allow more relaxed systems to emerge, not only must the environment and the space support free learning activities, but staff and, to a degree, the children's parents, must understand [the settings] culture and be in tune with its traditions'. Prochner et al. (2008) agree and suggest that the least mature system is one where direct teaching and 'school-like' activities take precedence over play. This presents a challenge to settings in considering where emphasis is placed within the systems already operating. The EYFS places great importance on policies and procedures to meet the learning and development legal requirements and welfare of children (DCSF, 2008f). Although this is an essential aspect of any early years setting, the way in which these systems are implemented and interpreted by practitioners determines the nature and value placed upon play. Consider your setting for a moment. To what extent is it driven by 'top down' policy outlined in the Statutory Framework of the EYFS? It is important to consider if your setting has become 'stuck in a rut' in complying with policy and legislation and is overlooking the creative possibilities within the statutory systems that govern the early years sector.

The setting in the case study had started to become stagnant in the way it provided play opportunities. Although it had a fantastic outside space and natural resources it had started to become overly concerned with risk assessment, limiting children's opportunity for free-flow play, creativity, and exploration. The introduction of the forest school started to change the focus of the setting as the combination of the natural environment and children's interests opened up a whole new stimulus of imaginative, creative, and investigative involvement for practitioners. The ethos within the systems started to shift to a more 'bottom-up' approach, led by placing the child at the centre of practice rather than letting policy and systems dictate what happened in the setting. Jill, a practitioner working alongside Sarah, noted:

> It is interesting to see how the setting has changed since we introduced forest school. As one of the leaders said, it is not about having the physical space to have a forest school but it's more of a philosophy, an ethos that you adopt. I have certainly bought into it because I can see the difference in the children and also in my colleagues. We are much more relaxed and confident in our practice and I think that is because we now understand how to use our policies to really support children in developing through play. (Interview, August 2009)

The practitioners in the setting realised that in providing play they needed to find a way of working that would offer a holistic experience for both the children and the way in which they approached play-based practice. This required them to analyse how they approached their outdoor and indoor space in order to create a flow between the two, even if they were not able to offer 'free-flow' play all of the time. The forest school has had a big impact on the setting in terms of the way practitioners use the environment as part of stimulating play experiences rather than seeing it as something necessary but separate from developing children's interests.

Continuous Professional Development Activity

There is limited research about taking a 'bottom-up' or child-centred approach that examines children's perspectives on their experiences in settings (Greene and Hill, 2005). However, some studies have examined the relationships between practitioners and children via observation of adult/child interaction and these agree that such relationships are important in measuring quality experiences for children (de Kruif et al., 2000; Melhuish, 2001). Gaining perspectives from children regarding their quality experiences in your setting may be challenging. Katz (1994) provides some guidance for deducing the perspectives of young children; for example, children will display a sense of acceptance, respect, and engagement in play. The nature of these qualities can be gathered from observing children as they move around within your setting's environment.

'Bottom-up' play environments *vs.* 'top-down' necessity

Aims

- To consider how you support a 'bottom-up' approach to children's play environments.

- To explore 'top-down' policy and procedure and how these translate into practice.

- To evaluate your practice and approach to play environments in supporting a 'bottom-up' perspective whilst working within 'top-down' parameters.

 Activity

1 Think about day-to-day practice in your setting. How much of what you do is 'top-down' driven – i.e. focused on maintaining policies and procedures which take precedence when working with children?

2 In contrast, evaluate how much of your practice takes a 'bottom-up' approach where practice evolves from the children's interests and ideas. Think about when the setting's environment is designed around the child and when you are creative in working within policy and procedures to provide child-led play.

3 The table below may help you to structure your thoughts. First, think about your planning and the play opportunities you provide for children in your setting. Then consider if these are influenced by a 'top-down' approach or 'bottom-up' perspective. Record your reasoning for this and then consider how your setting's environment supports this approach.

Table 8.1 Planning play opportunities

Play opportunity	Top-down/bottom-up approach	Justification	How does the environment support this?

4 When you have recorded five or six play opportunities that you provide for children analyse the balance between your evaluation of 'top-down' or 'bottom-up' approaches.

5 Discuss this with your colleagues and consider if your focus needs to change. Also discuss how you might raise issues about 'bottom-up' and 'top-down' perspectives at a team meeting.

Question to consider

• *Is it possible to focus on providing child-centred perspectives in your day-to-day practice?*

There is a fine balance to be struck between ensuring that children are safe and secure in your setting and allowing them to have the freedom to explore and learn within that environment. The EYFS advocates for both, yet as discussed in this chapter a 'top-down' approach may overwhelm setting practices. Greene and Hill (2005) discuss the importance of children's experience and how this can shape views and dispositions towards building positive relationships and unique qualities. They state that experience is socially mediated and therefore shared. Whilst experience can be interpreted by others it becomes related and interwoven when they then become part of the process. As a practitioner you become part of that process and through observing children's engagement with their environment and each other you are able to support them in understanding and negotiating their worlds. However, this requires the child to remain at the centre of practice and concentrating on how your setting can provide opportunities through the environment, resources and relationships you build to support individual qualities and development. It also requires a holistic view of the child, coupled with attention being paid to individual personalities, developmental needs and understanding. This can be challenging in a large setting, but by identifying themes that are of interest and following these through into interesting and stimulating play opportunities, as demonstrated through Sarah's approach in the case study, it is possible to sustain a 'bottom-up' perspective to practice.

Summary

This chapter has considered what challenge means in providing play opportunities for children by exploring 'top-down' and 'bottom-up' perspectives on practice. It has examined the resulting experience for children and how the environment can work with practitioners to provide stimulating opportunities for children's play to develop. It has considered the balance between outdoor and indoor environments and discussed issues surrounding quality play and using play types to facilitate and develop children's interests. Values regarding practice have been explored to identify what you do and how you provide it. Consequently play environments and how they work in practice is central in supporting a child-centred approach to play.

Inspiring Environments for Inspirational Play

Natalie Canning

Chapter Objectives

This chapter explores the way the environment can provide opportunities for children to engage in different types of play and feel a sense of ownership and empowerment in what they are doing. It considers the need for 'flexible environments' where children can use resources to satisfy their curiosity and self-expression. It examines how the environment is the foundation on which a spiral curriculum for play development is built incorporating risk taking and learning. It asks practitioners to be creative in facilitating a child-centred environment, consulting children so they remain at the centre of the process.

Creating inspiring places for play

The environment has a powerful effect on children's play. It can stimulate their senses, support their social and emotional development, and cultivate their desire to explore the world around them. But what makes a successful play environment? Firstly, it seems there is a need to perceive play as having an essential part within the structure and organisation of the setting. When this is coupled with support and direction provided by practitioners who are intuitive and sensitive to the play needs of children, it can lead to what Paley

(2005) suggests is sustained interest, where learning opportunities can be nurtured. Shackell et al. (2008), as well as Brown (2003), take this view further and explain that successful play spaces which support children's learning and development generally follow a number of principles. These include:

- *Play spaces designed to enhance the setting*

   It is essential that play spaces are considered from the viewpoint of the child and work with the indoor and outdoor space available. This may require creative solutions to utilise odd-shaped spaces and to think like a child when planning your resources. Children can provide solutions where adults struggle to see the potential. For example, a setting that had a large, built-in floor-to-ceiling cupboard which wasn't really used was transformed in consultation with the children. They removed the doors and created a 'tree' house, painting the back wall with a tree and using it as a quiet space.

- *A space that can be used in different ways*

   Play spaces should contain non-directive play equipment where children can control their play and where the environment stimulates their imagination and creativity. For practitioners, a space that is not 'fixed' allows flexibility for new themes to develop, children's interests to be followed, and restrictions (because of the environment) to be minimised. Resources that are versatile can enable practitioners to use their imagination in supporting different types of play. Different textures and sizes of material, cardboard boxes and scrap store items make great resources for role play, den making, and arts and crafts which do not envisage an end product and rely on children's inspiration.

- *An environment that can involve the community and generate ownership amongst children and families*

   An Early Years Professional (EYP) candidate recently recounted her experience of facilitating a 'growing' project which had begun from a discussion with children about what they had eaten for dinner. This led to examining where food came from, how it grew, and what it needed to do this. This resulted in the children preparing a vegetable plot in the setting, growing their own plants, involving their parents in growing seedlings at home and then bringing these into the setting, and selling the plants once they were harvested. The project supported the six areas of learning in the EYFS, but more importantly involved everyone associated with the setting in caring about how the plants were doing. It also generated a conversation between practitioners, parents and children, providing a link which crossed cultures and reigniting interest in how the setting was supporting their children's development.

Believing in a play environment

Providing enabling environments relies not only on the physical space and resources available, but also on practitioner attitudes to supporting children to realise their full potential. Practitioners are the way in which an environment becomes enabling through effective practice to support children in a setting's routine. Play may form only a small part of the day, but it relies on practitioner values and beliefs about how that play can be facilitated to ensure the experience is child centred. The effective practitioner, therefore, not only has to reflect on their personal values and beliefs but also on how these are transmitted into the setting's environment. For example, the setting in the case study was careful to recruit staff who had a love of the outdoors because they could actively encourage outdoor play whatever the weather. They planned to integrate the forest school into their practice and therefore wanted like-minded practitioners to support that transition. While having practitioners with different experiences and perspectives can provide a lively debate, the team needs to believe in the underpinning ethos of the setting for this to provide sustained opportunities for a 'bottom-up' approach to childcare. This means 'opening doors' for children to create new memories and experiences – a positive idea, but one that the EYFS guidance recognises may be difficult, especially if there are radically different values and beliefs within a team and also if some parents and even other professionals and senior management teams may need convincing (DCSF, 2008c). Such attitudinal change requires consultation, a careful evaluation of how children physically use the space available and listening to what they say about what they enjoy and dislike. This point is illustrated in through Sarah's comment:

> The arts and craft area of the setting has always been inside but we noticed that children were not really using the space in the way we envisaged. When we had the canopy put up outside, we decided to move the arts and crafts next to the door so that messy activities could go outside in most weathers and we found an improvement in children wanting to engage in this type of activity. The practicality of where the arts and crafts were located impacted on how it stimulated children's interest. I didn't realise how important that was. (Interview, August 2009)

Sarah reflected that the children were demonstrating their preferences about the location of the arts and crafts by not using it and fulfilling its potential. However, from an adult perspective the space provided typical craft and scrap store resources, it met health and safety requirements, and supplied enough space for children to develop their interests. Sarah discovered when the arts and crafts were moved that the new location provided more open-ended possibilities for children to explore. It stimulated their interests in experimenting with different materials because they had more freedom and room under the canopy in the outside space. It may be that flexibility in the outside space was not so easily noticed by practitioners. It could also be that it eased some aspects of day-to-day organisation. Sarah commented that she felt 'more at ease' when larger messy projects went outside as this limited the amount of disruption to the inside area. The environment played a significant factor in meeting the creative development aspect of the EYFS, which states that 'creativity emerges as children become absorbed in action and explorations of their own ideas, expressing them through movement, making and transforming things using media and materials such as crayons, paints, scissors, words, sounds, movement, props and make believe' (DCSF, 2008e: 104). The original space provided a limited opportunity for children to realise their own ideas, but being able to combine the inside and outside space broadened the possibilities for creative opportunities.

Flexible environments

A view held by many educationalists is that flexibility is the key to learning (Bruce, 2001; Whitebread, 2008). Broadhead (2004) suggests that children are very skilful at making and following their own rules in play and that they can understand the necessity of bringing order and structure to what they are doing so that it makes sense to them. Children will establish rules about props, roles, behaviours, and actions that may alter as the play develops, but they are dependent on the environment which contains and provides boundaries for play. Nicholson (1971) has argued that this is the theory of 'loose parts', where the environment is flexible enough to support the physical movement of materials so that children can express their creativity, curiosity, and interests in play. He explained 'in any environment, both the degree of inventiveness and creativity, and the possibility of discovery, are directly proportional to the number and kind of variables in it' (1971: 30). This means that the space and the practitioners within it both need to support the way in which children want to move resources around to meet their play needs. For example, in the case study setting the outside space under the canopy allowed a sandpit and water tray to be side by side. The children regularly requested to mix the two together and provision had been made for a third tray where this could be facilitated. Children had also asked if the dinosaurs could play in the sand or the water and by allowing this practitioners were supporting children's play needs and their exploration within the six areas of learning: for example, testing whether the dinosaurs could 'swim' i.e. float or sink provided children with opportunities to experiment and 'explore and investigate' the different properties located within Knowledge and Understanding of the World area of learning (DCSF, 2008e: 78).

Identifying the areas in your setting that are flexible and inflexible will require you to add another element to your holistic observations of children engaging with their environment. In addition, a flexible environment requires flexible plans so that if a child makes an exciting discovery it can be used to stimulate their interest and learning further. For example, in the case study the boys engage in problem solving when their ball gets stuck in the tree. They subsequently spent a long time talking about how they could solve the problem and try some of their ideas out. Sarah, the practitioner, could not have planned for this, but could capitalise on it by offering further challenges that would engage the children's problem-solving skills at a later date. She also used her observation for retrospective planning as just because she didn't foresee the amount of stimulus a ball stuck in a tree could create did not mean that she could not record and assess the boys' experiences and learning.

A spiral curriculum

Retrospective planning – namely considering what has happened in the past and applying it to the present and future – supports the concept of a spiral curriculum. Play is a way in which spiral curriculums can be facilitated as children revisit and build upon the skills they are practising (Bruner, 1972). The up and down schema that Jack engaged with in the case study is a good example of where a spiral curriculum can support children in developing his interest and skill. Through his play Sarah could identify periods when he practised up and down movement, when he was able to master a skill he had been working on, and when he revised that skill to the situation or environment he was in – for example, the up and down schema being transferred from the outside space to the wooded, forest school area. This spiral of practice, mastery and revision could be supported by Sarah through child-directed play as she observed from a distance and identified how Jack was playing and in adult/child interaction where she could plan more structured activities which would build on Jack's interest and skill. Bruner (1972) applies the principle that anything can be taught to children of any age providing it is presented to them in a way that is accessible and where they show interest and a motivation to want to learn. Play is one way that stimulates that interest for further investigation and different ways of practising the same skill. It could be argued that adults also engage in a spiral curriculum by reworking and developing ideas, practising skills and revisiting experiences. Indeed Donaldson (1978) argues that adults need to engage with a spiral curriculum because it represents the same kinds of logical errors and reasoning problems which occur on a daily basis!

A spiral curriculum allows us to think about approaching practice, planning, and assessment. The flexibility within it also supports the sometimes repetitive nature of play for skill development or for pure enjoyment. When play is revisited children are not only making cognitive links with what has gone before, but are also finding new ways to develop their thinking and imagination. Hughes (2001) argues that children need to have playmates where they have the space and time to use their environment to participate actively in play. Bruner (1966) recognises that play in this form is influenced by doing, collaborating, and reflecting on when personal agency (i.e. the means by which something is accomplished) belongs to the child and should be celebrated. An environment that provides these opportunities not just on an individual basis but also for groups of children and different age ranges can instill the foundations for inspirational play.

Supporting a 'child's world'

The way in which children use spaces available to them is important in maintaining their 'world' of play. Cohen and MacKeith (1991), when considering creativity and imagination, identify children as 'world weavers', but children will also demonstrate the same skills in play when they create imaginary worlds, suspend their reality, and create their own rules, logic and language for their play. Hutt (1979) developed three broad areas of play to reflect how children can use their environment to make meaning. She defined these as:

- *ludic play* – when children are using their imaginations, resources, and environment to create characters or situations which are important to them and reflect their mood and feelings, but which may not always be obvious to an adult observer;

- *epistemic play* – where children explore the world around them, their resources, and environment to make meaning from what they experience;

- *structured activities* – which may be comprised of games with rules or adult-led agendas.

When children have the time and space to develop ludic or epistemic play they will engage with different ways of seeing the world. Maslow (1971) concludes that the main function of play is to enhance the process of self-discovery and self-realisation. He argues that by engaging in imaginary worlds children can practise the skills necessary to deal with the external or real world. Winnicott (1971) uses play to understand the inner world of the child and argues that this is a way for children to express and make sense of their emotions. He argues that the play environment should provide a transitional space where children can feel safe to explore and work through their emotions. In the case study, Jack used the forest school environment to do just this. His parents' recent separation had meant that he felt out of control in many situations. Sarah used the forest school experience to empower him to learn new skills, take small risks, and be in control. MacMahon (1992) has focused on emotional wellbeing in play and has argued that the process of play can help children deal with difficult aspects of their lives or specific instances that have happened such as bereavement or a separation in the family. Children will often engage in ludic play when they are trying to understand their emotions because the imaginary world separates them from the reality of a situation. MacMahon has argued that in supporting children through aspects of therapeutic play practitioners can re-skill and empower them by providing a greater sense of wellbeing in a safe and contained environment.

Disruptions to a child's personal, social, and emotional development can mean that they display aggressive behaviour and show their own anger and frustration in play. Wood and Attfield (2005) suggest that supporting children to consider feelings and develop relationships can contribute to their empowerment and therefore develop an emotional literacy to underpin a positive self concept, self-esteem, and confidence. Sarah addressed this in the case study by facilitating a Circle Time session where the children could devise strategies to recognise and help each other when feeling upset or sad. Jack suggested that they could share their favourite toys and give each other a hug. Involving children in helping to understand different emotions and perspectives supports them in having ownership of situations and indicated to Jack ways in which he could cope with his feelings.

Consulting children about their play environments

Placing play at the centre of your thinking about the environment you offer to children in your setting will allow you the freedom to explore with children how they would wish to design their space. Involving and encouraging children to express their opinions will not only provide you with information on what they really think about your space and resources, but also with an opportunity for you to assess the six areas of learning embedded within the EYFS. Brown (2003: 58) argues that 'Children who have little control over their world inevitably have fewer positive experiences, which in turn slows the development of their self confidence ... children who lack confidence, are less likely to take risks or try out different solutions to the problems they encounter'. In the case study Sarah's setting had decided to consult with children on the outdoor space by using this strategy. They had asked the children 'If you could change the outside area, what would you do?' Their suggestions were voice recorded and illustrated through plans, pictures, and models, as well as involving the children physically showing practitioners what they wanted and using 'smiley face' opinion polls. Some of their feedback can be seen in the table below:

Table 9.1 – Children's ideas for the outside space

Area of learning	Children's suggestions
Personal, social and emotional development	'Have a path that goes to the end of the garden so the babies don't get lost'. 'A place to sit under the tree'. 'Keep the grass to run on and play with my friends'.
Communication, language and literacy	'A postbox for the birds so we can send messages to them'. 'A place to bury treasure, then we can draw a map to find it'.
Problem solving, reasoning and numeracy	'We need to put the bird table up and down so I can put the food on and then [pointing to the higher branches of the tree] it goes up there for their tea'. 'If you have a seat under the tree then I can't build dens – can't you take your own chairs?'
Knowledge and understanding of the world	'Can we grow lettuce for the slugs and snails?' 'When I went to daddy's house we had tea outside everyday, can we do that?' 'I want a big sandpit so I can dig big holes!'
Physical development	'Places to run'. 'Can we have a tree house?' 'This is the place to build dens because it's got a place to tie the cover to'.
Creative development	'Sparkles in the trees so it looks like stars in the day'. 'If you built the snails their own house then they wouldn't want to eat the lettuce'.

These conversations had a purpose that went beyond an exchange between children and practitioners – involving the parents as the children's comments, drawings, and models were displayed. They also reflected the children's capacity for creative and imaginative thinking, based on their previous experiences which echoed their family situations and cultural experiences of living in a rural farming community, and involved all staff in developing ways by which the inside and outside space could support the EYFS principles and areas of learning in play-centred practice. Rinaldi (2005) argues that researching with children is valuable in co-constructing a rich play and learning environment and certainly staff in the setting agreed that this had been their experience. Children's views offered a new way of looking at the space and an insight into what was important for the children in an enabling environment. Through this emerging values, empowerment, and a sense of ownership were shared between children and practitioners.

Continuous Professional Development Activity

This activity provides you with an opportunity to share with others how you would design an early years environment with a particular emphasis on how you would resource and design a play space. Your decisions may be based on your values and beliefs about play environments or on what you have observed children enjoying doing and playing with in your setting.

What is your inspirational environment?

Aims

- To explore your values and beliefs about children's play spaces.

- To examine how your decisions as a practitioner impact on the way children use the environment.

- To reflect on your role in providing an inspirational environment for children's play.

 Activity

1 Design and plan an early years environment which reflects your values and beliefs about children's play. You may want to do this in a creative way by drawing, making a model, or by making notes or developing a mind map of how you would organise the space. The following questions may help you:

- What does your environment look like?

- What does it feel like?

- Who will be in it?

- What makes it different from the environment you work in now?

- What makes it inspirational for you?

- Think beyond resources and consider light, space, texture, freedom, sound, air, and access for all.

2 Now think about how you would resource your space. Collect any items that represent your underpinning values and beliefs about play spaces. These might be easily to hand or in your bag or pocket: things such as a twig to represent trees or a bell to represent musical instruments or a mobile phone to represent access to digital technology. Consider the balance of the things you have collected, their visual impact, their texture, and their physical properties.

3 In small groups share with your colleagues why you decided upon certain items, what they represent, and why they are meaningful to your space.

4 Consider if you have designed and resourced your space around the child or around your own personal preferences. Is there a difference here and what might the implications be of your design for the child and the setting?

5 Provide a justification and rationale for your environment. Try to draw not only on your personal experience but also on your knowledge and understanding of early years environments, your theoretical influences, and your observations about what works well for children.

6 Consider your motives for the choices you made for the items you have collected. Have you focussed on the outside environment because you particularly enjoy being outside? Have you emphasised sensori-motor play because you believe it stimulates creativity?

Question to consider

- *Do children naturally want to play in your environment?*

This builds on the theme of designing play spaces from a child's perspective. A good starting point for this is to consider the five senses in evaluating what you have in your environment and how it could be improved. For example, from a child's perspective what does it look like? Is it over stimulating with bright colours on the walls? Are there children's pictures displayed at child height? Is there natural light in your setting and how could this be maximised? By posing some of these questions you will begin to develop a more enabling environment where children will feel comfortable in participating. Another way in which you can do this is consult with the children in your setting and ask them about what they like/dislike about it. You have designed the space based on adult necessities, but what works for the children? You might have realised some of the things that come up by observing them using the space, but in gaining their opinions you are not only developing more of a child-centred view but also developing their sense of ownership over the setting.

Summary

This chapter has considered how it is possible to support children in what they do, how they can 'own' their play space, and the importance of flexible environments and resources to satisfy children's curiosity and promote their inventiveness and creativity. The chapter has considered how a spiral curriculum can support play development and learning through practising and revisiting skills. It has looked at the way inspirational environments come from the underlying values and beliefs of practitioners in facilitating children to explore and be imaginative and creative in what they do and how they do it. Inspirational play depends upon your own perspective, imagination, and commitment to follow though on your ideas, but an enabling environment lies at the centre of making children's experiences meaningful and creating play memories.

Section 4

Learning and Development

'Learning and development recognises that children develop and learn in different ways and at different rates, and that all areas of learning and development are equally important and inter connected.' (DCSF, 2008f: 9)

Learning and Development

> ## Case Study: Going to the Moon
>
> Natalie Canning
>
> The children in this case study are aged between two and three and a half years old. It is based on a non-participant narrative observation of play in a preschool.
>
> Jenny is a NVQ level 3 qualified practitioner who works in a preschool setting. She enjoys supporting the children in their play, but is very aware that she needs to be invited into their games rather than her initiating play. Jenny enjoyed drama at school and is conscious that she can dominate play situations because of her enthusiasm if she is not careful.
>
> Katie and Jess are in the role-play area which has been set up as a travel shop. Katie is playing with a toy airplane, swooping it off the ground and holding it high above her head saying 'I am flying in the sky – to the moon!' Jess is sitting on the floor putting dolls' clothes into a toy suitcase as Katie moves around her. John and Ben are playing in parallel to the girls with the telephone, pretending to book a holiday. John turns to Katie and says 'I want to come to the moon!' Jess looks up and says 'Me as well', then gets up and reaches for the plane Katie is holding. John comes over to Jenny who has been observing the play close by and says 'We want to go to the moon'. Jenny, aware that she needs to ask open-ended questions to support the children's own creativity, says 'Great! What do you need to go to the moon?' Jess says 'Clothes' and Ben responds 'No – a hat, a space hat!'
>
> He runs off to the scrap material area and brings back a small cardboard box, which he puts on his head. Katie, Jess and John copy him and John also brings back a piece of material which he uses as a cape, announcing 'I am the captain'. Ben says, 'No! I have a better hat so I'm captain'. John replies, 'But I've got wings to fly', indicating his cape, 'So I'm driving the space ship – you can be second and help, ok? We need a ship, ok?' Ben thinks about this and then repeats, 'We need a space ship'. He goes over to the scrap material to look for something suitable, pulls out a few boxes,

but then rejects them, saying to himself 'Too small' as he tries to get inside one of them. Jenny asks, 'All ready? Where's your spaceship?' Ben comes back, 'Nothing there' pointing to the boxes out on the floor. John says 'Follow me troopers!' He leads them away from the role-play area to where there is more space – 'Climb in' says John, pretending to open a door and jump over an imaginary barrier. The others follow his actions until they are sitting on the floor with one behind the other, with cardboard boxes (space helmets) on their head. John shouts to Jenny – 'Can you shut the door Jenny?' She comes over and pretends to shut the door – 'All ready for take off Captain' she reports to John. Ben is pretending to flick imaginary switches and making clicking noises as he does so. Jess and Katie are behind Ben and Jess pretends to put her seatbelt on.

Jenny counts down from five to one in a loud voice and the children start to join in. They all shout out 'Lift off' while Jenny steps back and says 'Have a nice time!' John starts to lean back, pushing against Ben and making the others do the same, imitating the motion of lifting into the sky. Katie who is at the back of the spaceship reaches towards Jenny saying 'Come with us – I'm scared'. John and the others are making loud whooshing noises as they pretend to fly to the moon. Jenny pretends to run and jump into the spaceship and sits behind Katie. Jess, who is sitting in front of Katie, turns around and says 'Hold hands, Katie, be ok'. Jenny calls to John 'How long Captain until landing?' John begins to respond, but Rachel, another practitioner, calls out 'Snack time, everyone wash their hands!' The play stops almost immediately and although Jenny tries to pick up the theme again after the break, the children rotate to another play area.

10

Playing and Learning: Ways of Being in Action

Karen Appleby

Chapter Objectives

This chapter encourages practitioners to critically examine their personal perspectives on playing and learning and in particular to consider in more depth the role of children as players and learners. The focus is on developing children's dispositions to play and learn through practice that is informed by a knowledge and understanding of children's identities as players and learners. This requires practitioners to examine their assumptions about play and to recognise the challenges involved. Key themes introduced for this purpose include reflection on current debates and theoretical perspectives, examining the way play is conceptualised and learning about children as players and learners from observing and participating in their play.

Ways of being

In the quest for better outcomes for children (DfES, 2004) there is a danger that children's playing and learning are perceived as commodities that can be planned, controlled and measured to such an extent, that the essence of what it means to be a player and a learner is destroyed. It is important to tune into a child's identity as a player and learner in the here and now, understanding who they are and how they approach playing and learning in order to gain a deeper understanding of what is meant by children's 'interests', one that goes beyond a fascination with dinosaurs. What are the child's 'ways of being' and what is the relationship of these to 'states of being' as a player and learner? For example, in the case study when John responded to Katie's imaginative narrative about going to the moon, he demonstrated an interest in the idea of travelling to the moon, but the way in which he engaged with this interest was as someone who was aware of what was going on around him and could recognise the potential for developing an idea into further imaginary play. He demonstrated a disposition for developing a play narrative by using an idea provided by another child. John's way of being 'in action' was as a listener, a responder, and a social negotiator. We can only surmise that from his perspective this was an opportunity to be mentally and physically active, to be the leader of the play and the social group. Interpretating his actions can provide some insight into his 'state of being', including the cognitive, physical and emotional dimensions. In relation to the emotional dimension, it could be argued that John's state or frame of mind reflected motivation and social confidence within the play context. Later in the play he had the confidence to go to the practitioner and ask for support in developing the game. This insight into children's engagement in play goes beyond a superficial interpretation of a child's interests and can support effective participation in children's play as well as informing planning. The focus here is on understanding children rather than assessing them and on supporting their development as players and learners rather than on what they are learning as they play. Although the EYFS introduces key principles for practice there is a need to give further consideration to the nature and quality of children's experience. Developing children who are players and learners requires practitioners to understand and support who children are as players and learners. The following definitions can help clarify these perspectives:

- *Way of being in action:* Undertaking the role as a player and learner, represented by the child through their actions and potentially perceived in the same way by others.

- *Way of being:* Undertaking the role as a player and learner seen from a child's perspective.

- *State of being:* Physical, cognitive and emotional states experienced by a child in any one situation which can include states of mind and body.

Insight into children's identities as learners and players enables a skilled practitioner such as Jenny in the case study to facilitate learning journeys through sensitive and informed participation in play. This involves recognising when a child needs 'space' to enable them to assume control of their experience, when and how to participate, and when to provide support. Jenny ensured that the play remained child led, enabling them to assume different roles or ways of being in the play scenario, but also facilitated participation without controlling the play, providing her with the opportunity to observe, interpret, and respond appropriately. The nature of the children's engagement in the play suggested that she was nurturing their ways and states of being players and learners. In the case study the level of motivation and 'interest' in the trip to the moon might have been stimulated by the idea of being an astronaut and travelling in a spaceship, but helping children sustain and develop a play narrative requires a deeper understanding of their engagement with the experience.

Dispositions and habits of mind

Tuning into a child's identity as a player and learner can provide practitioners with an insight into children's dispositions or 'orientation towards the world' (Anning and Edwards, 2010: 7) and ways of nurturing positive approaches to playing and learning opportunities in the future. Arnold (2003) refers to dispositions as habits of mind which have a significant role in children's learning, while Anning and Edwards (2010) state that developing positive dispositions goes beyond being open to learning opportunities and includes children developing a positive sense of their own abilities and aptitude to learn. For this to happen, practitioners must value these aspects of a child's development and possess the skills and knowledge to nurture these in practice. The way a child approaches or responds to their world will be affected by a mixture of biological and socio-cultural factors with some aspects more established than others. A child's way of being in action may reflect an established disposition or habit of mind or an exploration of new possibilities led by others. Therefore understanding and responding effectively to a child's identity as a player and learner requires not only a knowledge of the individual built up over time but also an open mind and the capacity to be surprised by a child's response and to respond appropriately. A child's exploration of different ways of being may lead to the development of new dispositions and habits of mind and new ways of being a player and a learner. The role of play opportunities where children can build on and develop positive dispositions to learn can be seen in the case study when the children are actively co-constructing

(Vygotsky, 1978) and negotiating meaning with others (Wells, 1987). When Ben explored ways of representing a 'space hat' using resources he had found, he was demonstrating an 'orientation' towards imaginative play, an active exploration of his world (Piaget, 2001), possibility thinking (Craft, 2000), and problem solving. His self-appointed role was to find the resources for the props. He was also being a team member and collaborator. From one case study it would be impossible to judge whether Ben was demonstrating a 'habit of mind' or a new way of being. The emphasis however must be on gaining an insight into his approach and engagement with the experience. In contrast with this interpretation of dispositions, the EYFS conceptualises these in terms of 'understanding', 'learning' and 'awareness' implying that they are learning outcomes or products rather than an 'orientation' or way of being. It is possible to assess outcomes and this may explain why they are expressed in this way, but is it appropriate or possible to assess a child's orientation? And is it more appropriate to understand them?

Questioning practice guidance in this way requires a professional dis-position or orientation towards critical self-reflection and the confidence to challenge assumptions that inform the implementa-tion of the EYFS principles in practice. As Broadhead (2004: 131) argues, observing children is not sufficient here – we need to 'think and talk about understanding learning'. I would add that we also need to think and talk about understanding playing and the rela-tionship with learning. The EYFS provides practitioners with general guidance but high quality provision requires a deeper understanding of the child as a player and learner. Practice that is based on a nar-row and functional perspective on play, one that focuses on 'using' children's 'play' to achieve planned learning outcomes rather than on the nature and quality of the child's engagement, will compro-mise the central role of the child as a 'player' and 'learner' and ironically the 'outcomes' themselves. In the following quote the EYFS identifies a focus on achieving outcomes rather than on the need to understand a child's identity as a learner and player.

> By using the information on learning and development to support continuous observational assessment practitioners will form a view of where each child is in their learning, where they need to go, and the most effective practice to sup-port them in getting there. (DCSF, 2008: 12)

The EYFS provides basic guidance on how to work with and under-stand children's learning, but there is potential for a narrow and surface approach to its implementation if practitioners are unwilling to examine the content critically. Developing a deeper understand-ing of children's internal worlds, the motivation that drives their actions and interaction with the world and the sense they are making of their experience, is challenging. It requires practitioners to take responsibility for developing their professional knowledge and skills. It is important to move beyond the basic principles within the EYFS and to engage in current debates about playing and learning. You only have to visit the Nursery World forum or Open Eye campaign to access practitioner opinions about the implementation of the EYFS. Further to this, practitioners need to be aware of how particular theoretical perspectives can infiltrate debates and influence decisions and approaches to practice.

Current debate: perspectives on ways of being

Research evidence from neuroscience has encouraged an emphasis on brain development and a belief that young children must be exposed to an 'enriched' environment (Smidt, 2006: 124). There is a concern that the adult may be perceived as responsible for this and as a consequence must assume control of the learning experience, believing that every learning opportunity must be utilised. Whilst recognising the importance of stimulating experiences, Blackmore and Frith (2007: 32–33) warn of the potential but as yet unknown effect of over-stimulation on the brain. They emphasise that a 'normal child centred environment' will provide sufficient sensory stimulation. In their view the adult should be leading or directing less, thereby creating more time for observing children whilst they are playing and making informed decisions about when to intervene and extend learning and when to wait to be invited by the child. The case study is a good example of this as Jenny the practitioner facilitated the children in child-centred play where the stimulation and imaginative play came from the children.

For Trevarthen (2009) the current focus on developing cognitive functions of the brain ignores the important role of the emotional brain. He believes that a child's brain is wired in such a way as to pick up meanings, motives and feelings of others and that it is the role of the cognitive dimension to serve this purpose, not the other way around. Trevarthen (2004: 31) argues that 'our conceptions of sympathetic and intuitive mental life have become over cognitive and impoverished'. Therefore it is important to recognise and tune into children's interests through their emotional responses, ways of being, and states of mind. He reminds us that human states of mind are communicated through behaviours. In the case study Jenny, the practitioner, tuned into Katie feeling scared (her state of mind) about the journey to the moon. Katie had the disposition to imagine, otherwise she wouldn't have been scared, and Jenny was facilitating her way of being as a player. Katie was engaged in imagining she was an astronaut, opening up possibilities for her to explore new ideas in conjunction with the other children. She wanted to participate in this experience but it involved her being a risk taker, a process that is important as an orientation to learning. Through Jenny's actions in supporting Katie whilst remaining in the imaginary play she enabled her to access her zone of proximal development (ZPD) (Vygotsky, 1978). ZPD provides a 'foundation for joint activity where the practitioner can lead the child ahead of his or her development' (Wood and Attfield, 2005: 96). In the context of the case study, ZPD was being used to create a capacity for further imaginary play, emotional responses, creativity, and the opportunity to explore and communicate ideas. This demonstrated that ZPD has relevance outside an outcome-driven view of learning.

Theory can offer us some insight into a child's perspective but can never provide us with the whole picture of what is happening inside the brain and mind. Practitioners can only interpret children's internal processes through the ways they represent and communicate these 'in action' through what they say and do. Your ability to interpret children's behaviour, responses and understanding is limited, however articulating and discussing the complex processes involved is one way of building a shared understanding. Consequently, examining and developing how you use language to understand children as players and as learners is an essential aspect of continuing professional development.

Examining the language of play and playing

The term 'playing' is used here to make the distinction between play as a product – something that can be observed, categorised or labelled – and 'playing' as a child's 'way of being' and how these are represented in action. It is important to articulate these differences because the nature of the language used within published texts and the EYFS to discuss children's behaviours and to inform and guide practice can in itself create a challenge for practitioners. A critical examination of this language can support a clearer understanding of some of the key issues related to children's roles as players and learners and the role of the adult within this process. The use of the term 'play' is particularly confusing as it is used as a verb to describe a child's role as well as a noun to label and categorise the behaviours and experiences associated with that role (Moyles, 2005).

Table 10.1 Play language

Verbs		Nouns		Examples of language use
to play	playing	player	play	Verb or noun?
				'Play underpins all development and learning for young children' (DCSF, 2008e: 7).
				Noun (categorising and labelling):
				• Role play.
				• Imaginative play.
				• Socio-dramatic play.

The range of language used to conceptualise and discuss children's play is likely to affect our ability to develop a deeper understanding of what is involved and may encourage an emphasis on product disassociated from the nature and quality of a child's experience. To further illustrate this point it is interesting to consider the phrase 'play is children's work' (Meadows, 1986) and to note that in common with the term 'play', 'work' is used by some as a verb and a noun. This association may encourage an assumption that play (playing) can be categorised, labelled, seen and understood in the adult world, rather than being perceived as an action of freedom, creativity and choice owned by the child. For Broadhead (2004: 89) play 'is far more than this. Play is their self-actualisation, a holistic exploration of who they are and know and who and what they become'. This implies a much more complex process, aspects of which may be observed and labelled but with much happening below the surface and driven by internal forces. In contrast with this perspective a definition of play as child's work places an emphasis on observable tasks or activities rather than on a way of being as a player with associated dispositions or habits of mind. A significant challenge for you as a practitioner is recognising how you can control and manage what children are doing in the concrete sense of 'work'. This is much easier than understanding and facilitating children's ways of being as players. It is also much harder to 'see' the benefits of this approach because the control and autonomy lie with the child to a greater extent.

Playing and learning

Play is conceptualised within the EYFS in terms of how children learn and therefore encourages practitioners to value, understand,

and describe play within this framework. This approach is further supported by theories which identify the role of play in children's learning. Consequently the relationship between playing and learning is further reinforced through the concepts and associated language used to describe children's playing. The nature of this relationship can make it difficult for practitioners to conceptualise playing and learning as distinct but inter-related ways of being, to value play beyond the purpose of learning, and to recognise that playing is far more than a tool for learning. Understanding the differences is just as important as understanding the synergy. A key difference is that the role of the learner can be stimulated and controlled by others through adult-led activities whilst the role of a player is initiated and controlled by the child. The child chooses to play and to be playful. A key similarity is that it is possible to plan opportunities for both playing and learning but the actual nature and quality of the experience are dependent on how the child responds. Play in the case study was initiated and developed by the children, supported by Jenny's sensitive participation that enabled each child to assume different ways of being a player and learner as the narrative unfolded. Within the EYFS both adult-led activities and child-initiated experiences are presented as part of a play-based curriculum, implying that it is possible to manage children's play experiences. Once again the use of language reflects a need to clarify further significant concepts about playing and learning.

A greater examination of children's 'ways and states of being' within play scenarios can provide practitioners with an opportunity to develop a deeper understanding of significant concepts about playing and learning and the relationship between these. Developing a register of language based on observation will support an identification and understanding of children's responses and how to respond to these in practice. For example, in the case study John assumed the role of leader, enabling himself and others to use their imagination, to explore possibilities and develop their ideas. His role as player and learner was indistinguishable, reflecting the synergy between playing and learning. Further analysis of the case study and the children's responses could highlight their ways of being in action, as well as an interpretation of their perspective and their states of being as players and learners.

Ways of being in action included being;

- explorers;

- thinkers and meaning makers;

- imitators;

- communicators;

- possibility thinkers (Craft, 2000);

- creators;

- decision makers;

- motivators;

- leaders;

- observers;

- listeners;

- learners.

From the child's perspective they were possibly being:

- players;

- astronauts;

- passengers;

- part of the social group;

- participants in a story.

To engage in this way they demonstrated the following states of being:

- mentally and physically active;

- in control;

- focussed;

- involved;

- socially confident;

- curious;

- motivated;

- purposeful;

- imaginative;

- creative;

- anxious.

Children may demonstrate these ways and states of being within free play and structured activities led by an adult. These would both constitute contexts for learning (but as discussed earlier) not necessarily contexts for playing. Within an adult-led activity there is the potential for a child to become a player, but the practitioner has to recognise the potential for playing within the activity and 'tune into' and respond appropriately to the child's initiative. This requires practitioners to work with the ebb and flow of human behaviours and responses, to 'reflect in action' (Schön, 1987) as was demonstrated by Jenny's participation in the play scenario. This requires practitioners to engage in a process of 'possibility thinking' (Craft, 2000), to respond with an open mind to different ways of understanding playing and learning. It also requires thinking divergently about evidence from experience and reading and then formulating and articulating new insights which in turn can inform practice.

Ways of being in action

Developing a deeper understanding of children's engagement as players and learners requires new ways of thinking and talking about playing and learning. The diagram below illustrates an approach which highlights the significance of the child's brain, body and mind and how each element can affect the other when playing and learning. For example, in the case study Ben used his thinking skills to identify that they needed 'space hats' and appropriate resources; his physical skills enabled him to collect the materials and to make a helmet from a cardboard box, but he also needed the drive and motivation to carry out his intentions.

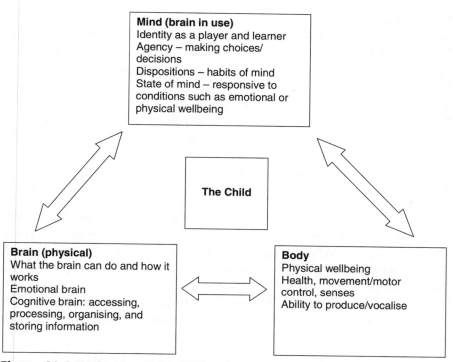

Mind (brain in use)
Identity as a player and learner
Agency – making choices/
decisions
Dispositions – habits of mind
State of mind – responsive to
conditions such as emotional or
physical wellbeing

The Child

Brain (physical)
What the brain can do and how it
works
Emotional brain
Cognitive brain: accessing,
processing, organising, and
storing information

Body
Physical wellbeing
Health, movement/motor
control, senses
Ability to produce/vocalise

Figure 10.1 Understanding children's ways of being in action

It is helpful here to use a metaphor to explain this model. Consider the role of the child as player and learner in the context of being the driver of a car. The driving which is observed by others will be affected by the driver's cognitive framework, perception and processing skills (brain functions), sensory capacity and motor co-ordination (physical attributes). What must also be considered and can be forgotten is the way in which the individual perceives their role as a driver, their identity and disposition to drive as well as their emotional, cognitive and physical wellbeing (state and habits of mind). All of these factors are important and can affect each other. Having the requisite cognitive and physical potential is not enough – the individual must make the choice to drive, the child to play and learn. Either consciously or unconsciously they control their engagement with the task. This may be through an intrinsic love of driving but it may also be at times because they have a destination in sight, a genuine purpose for the journey. A lack of confidence, feeling tired, or having had a bad experience can, however, affect motivation and the nature and quality of the driving experience.

It is possible to manipulate someone into driving, as it is to control to some extent a child's learning, but the individual's emotional wellbeing, their state of mind including their motivation, will affect the nature of the experience and consequently what happens as a result. Physical wellbeing, levels of concentration, confidence, self-esteem, and the individual's identity as a driver (learner or player) will all be factors affecting the nature of the experience and the outcome. A key point to make here, though, is that once the choice has been taken away from the individual, their way of being will no longer be playful and this will be reflected in their way of being in action; the driver or child will no longer be playing although they may still be learning. This can be related to the experience of learning to drive. It is also important to remember that all of this is happening within a physical, social and cultural context and that the child's mindset, their ways and states of being, will be affected by these factors. Cultural tools, such as the nature of the physical environment available to the child and how they respond to these resources, represent one example of how external factors can impact on the child. In this sense, understanding the child as a player and learner must take into account any previous experience as a player and learner as well as the context in which they are operating. It is essential that practitioners recognise the effect of different conditions on a child's ways of being in action.

It also important to recognise the range of ways whereby children might engage with their world and that as well as initiating ways of being they will also respond and interact with their environment. In this sense their ways of being are not 'fixed'. Within an adult-initiated activity a child may be given the space to be a player, to take control of their experience on their own terms, but equally, adult participation in a child's free play may change the nature of the child's engagement and ways of being in action. Therefore the ability to identify the nature of a child's player and learner identity within any one context, to work flexibly, reflect 'in action' and make informed responses, is a significant quality in an early years practitioner. The case study does not focus on Jess, but reflection on her experience of 'going to the moon' could lead Jenny to provide different play opportunities in which she is able to play a more active role. It is important to consider why these aspects of children's playing and learning experiences should be explored. Although it is not possible to analyse and understand every child's responses in depth, engaging in this process can support a deeper understanding of children's needs, making it is possible for them to have the space and support necessary to be players and learners, and enabling them to explore and develop new ways of being, dispositions, and habits of mind.

Continuing Professional Development Activity

This chapter has considered some of the theoretical underpinnings relating to ways of being in action, as well as habits and dispositions of learning and states of being. This activity can support you in putting these perspectives into practice. It is a tool for analysing and learning from children's playing and learning experience, viewing their playing and learning as a fluid interchange for further development.

Analysing children's playing and learning experiences

Aims

- To develop practitioner use of language to identify, analyse, and evaluate children's roles as players and learners.
- To support a deeper understanding of playing and learning.
- To inform future practice.

 Activity

Part 1

1 Think about your practice and identify and label children's different ways of being players and learners in action; for example, children's behaviours that you have observed in free play such as the child being an explorer, a role player, a talker, or an observer. You may find it useful to discuss and record these with a colleague.

2 Record your ideas on the top section of the 'iceberg' (Figure 10.2) to represent the observable features of children's roles as players and learners.

3 Consider what is going on for children when they are engaged in these roles. These are the hidden ways of being that can inform our interpretation and understanding of children's play. Try to imagine yourself in the role of the child.

4 Record these in the middle section of the 'iceberg' to represent the child's perspective, their way of being.

5 Next consider the factors from within the child which may affect their behaviours and responses.

6 Identify potential drivers for children's observable behaviour, for example, curiosity, assertiveness or a need for physical activity.

7 Record these in the bottom section of the 'iceberg' to represent potential states of being.

8 In the box underneath the 'iceberg' list possible playing and learning dispositions or habits of mind.

9 Finally consider factors within the environment which may affect children's responses and record these outside of the 'iceberg'.

You have now created a framework for analysing and reflecting on children's playing and learning.

Part 2

Experiment using the iceberg tool you have created to reflect on children's play. It should not be used as a tick list or method of assessment, but as you use the tool identify any gaps and add further descriptors.

Part 3

Use the tool to reflect on children's identities as players and learners and to consider implications for your practice.

Question to consider

- *What impact has this activity had on the way you think about children as players and learners – will it inform your practice?*

  Initially you may have found it challenging to engage with different perspectives, but applying these principles to real examples from your own practice will enable you to make sense of these perspectives for the children in your care. It is important to reflect on how you view children as players and learners and whether your own views impact on how you approach your practice. Interpreting what you observe and considering the processes of playing and learning are vital for developing your own professional practice and engaging with your setting in developing a ethos where there is a balance between both playing and learning and where a shared understanding starts to emerge.

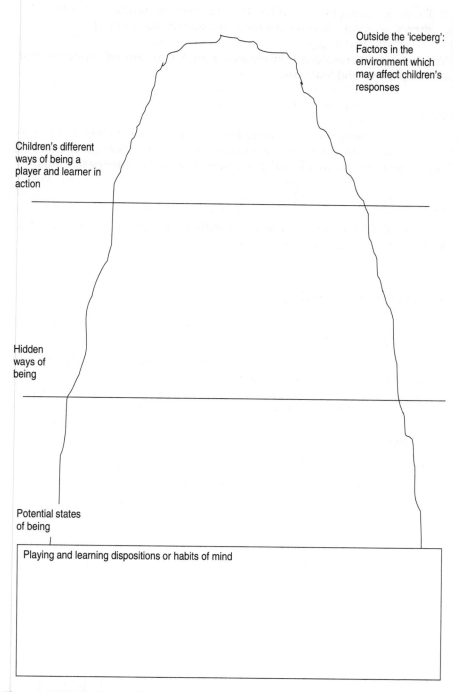

Figure 10.2 Iceberg diagram

Summary

The focus of this chapter has been on children as players and learners and the development of a professional disposition or orientation to understanding children's worlds. The purpose has been to challenge current ways of thinking about playing and learning, about how play in particular is conceptualised and articulated, including the way it is presented within the EYFS. Practitioners also need to consider what they need to learn, how children learn, and how best to support them (Anning and Edwards, 2010). Understanding and nurturing young children's identities as players and learners, however, is the key to children recognising their own abilities and learning how to use and develop these. They need to learn how to learn for themselves if they are to achieve their full potential.

11

Creative Play for Flexible Learning

Natalie Canning

Chapter Objectives

This chapter examines creativity in the context of the play environment. It explores definitions of creativity and considers the importance placed on creative processes as a holistic approach to developing creativity in children. It also examines the role of the practitioner in supporting creativity in a setting and working within the practice guidance of the EYFS and considers how children can develop creative dispositions and behaviours through their experiences and how they express these through play.

Creativity in a play context

As with play there has been much debate as to how creativity is characterised and defined (Duffy, 2006). Perceptions of creativity vary according to individual experiences and a personal interpretation of what being creative means and what it involves. Rogers (2000) argues that for any creativity to emerge there needs to be a nourishing and nurturing environment, where there is a culture of openness to new concepts and a tolerance for ambiguity. In the same way, play opportunities also require these characteristics to enable children to explore and follow their own interests. Play and creativity are closely related because through children's exploration and curiosity they engage with creative processes: for example, trial and error, using imagination, or engaging in symbolic play where an object is imagined as something else, i.e. a stick becomes a wand or (as in the case study) a cardboard box becomes a space helmet. Rogers also argues that creative connections are made when children play, stimulating self-expression and building opportunities for links to be made to extend opportunities for different ways and states of being as discussed in the previous chapter. Consequently creativity is more than the arts and crafts corner – it comes from within the child, their self-expression and emotional connections with people and the environment.

The EYFS states that 'creativity is about taking risks and making connections and is strongly linked with play' (DCSF, 2008e: 104). It is interesting then that the practice guidance identifies 'creative development' as one of the six areas of learning whilst play is considered to underpin what happens in all practice. Play and creativity are interrelated so if play is seen as something that permeates through all practice then creativity must also be seen in the same way. If creative development is one area of learning in the EYFS then it may translate into practice as something that will stand alone. But it is difficult to compartmentalise creativity because for children it connects with play and is not something that is tangible or able to be measured – it 'differs according to an individuals experience' (Duffy, 2006: 17). This can be problematic when working with the EYFS, as trying to understand a child's state of being, their physical, cognitive and emotional states when they are engaged in creativity, relies on your interpretation. Seeing 'creative development' as one area of learning can narrow this interpretation and how practitioners view creative opportunities. This can have a detrimental impact on practice because creativity is being measured using a 'tick list' mentality rather than an emerging process which belongs to the child. In the case study the creativity in the play permeated via the children's engagement with each other and how they developed the play together. Jenny, the practitioner, recognised this and was creative in her own responses to the children, remaining in the imaginary role of 'going the moon'. The play and creativity co-existed to support the children's interests, learning, and development.

Supporting the creative potential

Rogers adopts humanistic principles of creativity which consider that everyone has an innate ability to be creative, a process that develops with new experiences and mastering new skills. The view that creativity is a universal capability (Lowenfeld and Brittain, 1987; Duffy, 2006) suggests that opportunities for creative engagement need to be nurtured. In the same way, Wyse and Downson (2009) identify that while everyone may have the capacity to be creative they may not have the same potential to demonstrate this. If play can offer opportunities for creative development to occur children will begin to build a foundation on which creativity can become embedded into their childhood experiences. Duffy (2006: 17) suggests that there is a continuum of creative competence which provides a framework where individuals can be viewed as being creative whilst demonstrating different levels of creativity. This continuum has at 'one end highly creative geniuses' such as Picasso, and at the other, everyday creativity such as problem solving. In the case study Ben engaged with creative problem solving when he searched through the scrap materials to consider the possibilities for space helmets, rejecting several items before he settled on small cardboard boxes. Craft (2000: 3) refers to this type of creativity as 'little c creativity', based on everyday interactions which will generate creative ways of doing or seeing things. Children constantly demonstrate 'little c creativity' in their play, unaware that they are engaging in a creative process which supports their thinking and learning. At the other end of the scale, Craft identifies 'big C creativity' to describe the work of creative geniuses. This is the type of creativity that adults generally think of and make judgements and generalisations about whether they have any creative ability. Adults tend to look for an end product that 'proves' someone has been creative, rather than considering the process of engaging with different ideas or trying things out.

The debate surrounding creative definitions also refers to the idea that to be creative a product or outcome must contribute to a 'purposeful activity directed to achieving an objective or generating something original' (NACCCE, 1999: 31). The ambiguity within this relates to how originality and purposeful activity are defined. When considering creativity within an early years setting practitioners have to consider not only the nature of children's creative processes, but also the relationship between this, a potential end product and a judgement about it's originality. An end product may emerge in a number of forms such as a physical model, an imaginary role play, or solving a problem. In the case study the product was the play narrative that was constructed between the children. There are also different interpretations with regard to what originality means within creativity. Robinson (2001) describes creativity as producing outcomes that are completely new and not copied or coming from something else. In today's society this is difficult to achieve, but Vernon (1989) argues for a more individual view of originality in that creativity is a person's capacity to produce new ideas for themselves. This means that children are able to discover something new to them for the first time and for this to still be considered original. Gardner (1997) views originality as children asking questions to stimulate their curiosity and Bartlett (1959, cited in Fisher, 2004: 13) refers to originality as 'adventurous thinking to break out of a mould' and discover something different or new. In the case study Jenny, the practitioner, reflected that John could have been demonstrating originality in his play through his adventurous thinking about going to the moon. She considered how the children asked questions of John through the play and how significant this was as an indicator of the emerging play narrative as a creative product. She judged this by considering if the play was purposeful to the children and reflected that it was. As with play it is important to evaluate the quality processes involved in creativity and whether any value should be given to 'originality' or to a resulting product or end outcome. This decision should be evaluated in terms of who needs physically to have an end product – the child, the practitioner, Ofsted inspectors or the EYFS requirements – and the implications for not having an end product.

An outcome-driven attitude towards creativity encourages a narrow approach to structuring creative opportunities because you are looking for the outcome. This can potentially limit experiences by focusing on individual elements rather than viewing play and creativity as a holistic interaction. In focussing on one area of development, a practitioner might inadvertently be blocking opportunities for children to achieve their creative potential by not allowing them to take a more flexible approach. In supporting open-ended play opportunities you are also enabling creative opportunities. This is something that is difficult to anticipate or plan for and must come from the child's engagement in the play context. Fisher (2004) advocates for creativity to be seen as three separate elements which include both the process and product:

- Children can develop creative property where creativity becomes integrated into what children do, as well as their attitudes, beliefs, and approach to play. This element supports Rogers' (2000) view of a humanistic approach to creativity.

- Children can engage with a creative process through what they do as part of everyday life, from problem solving to decision making. This supports Craft's (2000) view of 'little c creativity'.

- Creativity can be celebrated in terms of producing an end outcome or product. This can also relate to producing something of original value either personally or publicly and relates to the debate surrounding what is valued as creative merit.

Although Fisher's view may provide a way by which we can see different dimensions of creativity, it is more complex where the elements intertwine and are dependent upon each other. For example, in the case study the children used elements of creative property and the creative process to develop their imaginary play and these became difficult to separate as the scenario developed. The play generated a narrative which provided an individual learning experience that they could build upon in their next play encounter. For Katie this would be the support she would know she would receive not only from her friend, Jess, who showed empathy by holding her hand when she was scared of 'taking off', but also from Jenny, who supported her in the play.

Developing creative dispositions

To support creativity further Fisher (2004) argues that a number of factors need to be in place. These not only refer to the physical environment to provide stimulus for creative thinking but also to the attitude of practitioners in fostering a creative atmosphere or ethos in the setting. For creative dispositions to emerge, Rogers (2000) argues that time and space need to be given for children to engage in creative processes. These need to include a holistic approach where the practitioner is willing to follow the child's lead, not always knowing what the child's intention may be. This is supported to some extent by the EYFS, which states that 'being creative involves the whole curriculum, not just the arts. It is not necessarily about making an end product such as a picture, song or play' (DCSF, 2008d). Setting up an environment where there is time to explore and experiment with different materials is one of the core conditions for supporting creativity. Fisher identifies that another comes through providing a questioning environment where children have to find things out for themselves and must experiment and explore in order to find answers or solutions. In the case study, Jenny allowed the children to do this by standing back from the play and only engaging when invited to do so by the children. The resources were flexible enough to support the children in problem solving and engaging in imaginary play. Jenny was allowing the children to think for themselves and develop creative solutions to the problems the play presented as the 'going to the moon' plot became more complicated. She asked questions and sustained shared thinking between the children and herself by ensuring the conversation stayed in context to the play. The environment was nurturing the creativity generated by the children, but Jenny was extending not only the creative process by sustaining the play with her involvement, but in following the child's lead she was also developing their dispositions towards being creative learners. The EYFS states that 'sustained shared thinking can only happen when there are responsive, trusting relationships between adults and children' (DCSF, 2008d) and this was illustrated by the way Jenny supported Katie when the 'spaceship' was about to take off.

Crucial to the creative process is the emotional environment created in the setting. Children need to feel valued and accepted for themselves where the environment supports and excites them enough to express their feelings and unique qualities. An aspect of creativity is about making meaningful connections and using ideas and resources in new ways. This not only supports sharing experiences with others, but also widens children's ability to feel able to participate. Children need practitioners to support them in these processes, enabling them to develop skills and explore their own level of mastery. You can do this as a practitioner by:

- organising children's access to creative and imaginative opportunities through ensuring there are appropriate and flexible resources, space, and time to develop children's ideas and themes;

- organising your own role as a practitioner, considering how you will make observations of children to facilitate their creativity, whilst recording and making judgements about their levels of concentration, interest, shared understanding, and identifying what the child is doing to plan for future relevant play opportunities;

- developing creative dispositions which include being open to taking risks, using your imagination, and engaging in possibility thinking.

Creative behaviours

Csikszentmihalyi (1997: 1) explains that 'creativity is a central source of meaning in our lives ... most of the things that are interesting, important and human are the results of creativity'. This means that creativity must have a central role in children's lives and be encouraged so that this natural 'inner resource' is not lost as more formal and structured learning is introduced as children get older (Edgington, 2002). Developing dispositions to creativity supports children's confidence, self-esteem, motivation, and ultimate achievements because they are not afraid of 'having a go', experimenting in their play and in more formal learning situations. The QCA (2004) recognise that when children think creatively they become more open to new ideas and more interested in discovering things for themselves. The QCA (2004: 9) identify this as developing 'creative behaviours' that intrinsically link with play opportunities which can offer children the freedom and choice to explore and experiment. The Reggio Emilia philosophy works on the same principles where children are able to follow their interests that are organised and negotiated between children and a pedagogue (equivalent to a practitioner). The curriculum is then based around flexible themes and children are encouraged to engage with creative behaviours. In practice this means projects develop over a period of weeks, with resources and half-constructed creations being left so children can return, develop, and change these over time. Dispositions towards learning become intertwined with those of play, creativity, communication, and social engagement. Some settings in England have adopted similar principles and try to weave these into working with the EYFS. Aspects of the practice guidance support this by advocating 'sufficient time for children to explore and develop ideas and finish working through these ideas' (DCSF, 2008: 105) whilst then presenting the challenge of 'ensuring that children develop understanding of the importance of tidying up and putting things back where they belong' (DCSF, 2008d).

Another disposition towards creativity is possibility thinking. Craft (2001) argues that this is at the core of creative learning where children engage with problem solving by being encouraged to ask 'What If?' questions. The practitioner is central to facilitating possibility thinking through:

- posing relevant questions that are appropriate to the context of the situation;

- understanding children's unique qualities and how these can be supported in play to develop their confidence in exploring creativity;

- supporting children to make connections with others including adults who are flexible and willing to engage and explore creative responses to questions or experiences;

- using imagination to discover new ways of seeing or doing things and to bring learning opportunities to life;

- supporting children to take personal risks in trying something new or different or by expressing emotions and opinions (Burnard et al., 2006).

Fisher (2004) argues that there are rich resources and opportunities to practise possibility thinking as creativity starts from engaging in everyday activities and routines. Often the tasks that occupy these routines can overload practitioners ability to be creative, but possibility thinking does require you to ask the 'What If' questions in relation to providing a more dynamic and creative response to the structure of the day. For example, in the case study the play came to an abrupt halt when Rachel, the other practitioner stopped the children's play for snack time. What would have happened had she not done this? What if snack time had turned into 'space food' on the moon? Multiple opportunities could have been extended if the practitioner had employed possibility thinking and considered flexible ways of applying the daily routine to the children's needs and interests.

In the case study the 'creative capital' of the situation was not assessed (Fisher, 2004). This refers to the total resources needed to support a creative process and potential learning situation. It involves evaluating yourself as a practitioner, your role in the play situation, and the power you exert in directing play, stimulating creative processes, or potentially limiting them. It also requires an overview of the environment and resources, assessing how flexible these are in providing creative opportunities for different types of play to develop or co-exist in the same play space. Finally, it considers how children can develop partnerships with other children, how they can share creative experiences and can expand on ideas so that a shared understanding can be developed and sustained within a play context. These elements ensure that creativity is not left to chance or relies on 'an inherent drive and need to express' creativity (Rogers, 2000: 12), but instead enhances and channels the creative potential into creative production (Fisher, 2004).

Expressing creativity

The way in which children express and use creativity is dependent upon the cultural influences they experience. A socio-cultural context supports interaction between thoughts and actions and knowledge and skill. This has an impact on what and who are defined as 'creative' and what is valued in terms of creativity as a process or as an end product. Craft (2003) highlights the tensions practitioners may feel not only in providing for creative opportunities in a setting but also in recognising what creative learning looks like. Loveless (2005) suggests that being creative, developing ideas and turning them into something meaningful relies on making judgements about the value of creative thinking and the importance

placed on process-driven play. It involves translating the expectations of creativity in the EYFS into practice. The practice guidance in
relation to creative development states:

- creativity emerges as children become absorbed in action and
  explorations of their own ideas;

- creativity involves children in initiating their own learning and
  making choices and decisions;

- children's responses to what they see, hear, and experience
  through their senses are individual and the way they represent
  their experiences is unique and valuable;

- being creative enables babies and children to explore many
  processes, media and materials and to make new things emerge as
  a result (DCSF, 2008e: 104).

In working with these statements and turning them into reality for
children the practitioner has to make judgements about how they
are going to plan, observe, assess and implement them in practice.
This will depend on the cultural emphasis placed on creativity
within the setting and the immediate community of parents/carers
or grandparents. Trevarthen et al. (2008) uses the creative properties
of nursery rhymes as an example and argues that in singing them it
is important to understand the impact of timing, the feeling for
pitch and the sense of emotion and movement that can be
expressed. Different families may use different words, think that they
mean different things, and sing these in different ways because they
have been passed down from generation to generation and so will
deliver them in a way that is familiar to them. Trevarthen et al.
(2008) explains that apart from the creative and cultural potential,
nursery rhymes act as communication, encouraging children to
share in actions, expressions of energy and feeling in movement and
sound. This stimulates brain development, specifically cortical learning which relies on experiences and emotions to generate growth.
Consequently they consider that 'during early childhood learning is
quickest, most artistically inventive and most seductively sociable'
(Trevarthen et al., 2008: 7). This is apparent in the case study as the
imaginative scenario is quickly adopted by the children, the plot is
developed and children who might not normally play together are
included in the pretend play. As a result it is important that as a practitioner you recognise how you support children to develop these
skills and the value you place on creative processes within the culture of the setting and wider community. Trevarthan et al. advocate

for two principles in achieving this – one whereby practitioners believe children are 'natural artists and inventors, natural poets and musicians', and the other where children 'gain strength of understanding and new ideas best by acting and learning in the company of sympathetic (like minded) companions' (Trevarthan et al., 2008: 7). They place an emphasis on the importance of children developing friendships through play and engaging in creative opportunities such as imaginary play. By believing in these two principles, Trevarthan et al. argue, creativity can flourish in any setting.

Continuous Professional Development Activity

This CPD activity draws on activities that you may have completed in other chapters. It focuses on analysing the creativity that children engage in and requires you to involve children in an observation of their play. You will need to do some preparatory work before you start, to get the most out of the observation and ensure that you can carry out this activity within the realms of your setting's policy for consent and confidentiality.

Observing Creativity

Aims

- To identify the creative process that children engage with through play.

- To consider what constitutes creative behaviours and how children engage with open-ended resources to meet their creative needs.

- To explore if creativity is a inherent part of play.

 Activity

Part 1

1 Find a space in your setting that you can use to carry out an observation.

2 Try and clear the space as much as you can so that you can observe children's free choice of play and how they develop the space to meet their needs.

3 Pre-prepare and collect together open-ended resources (you could refer back here to the activity in Chapter 3 to remind yourself of what you identified as open-ended resources).

4 Consult with children on how they would like to fill the space. Offer them the opportunity of open-ended resources and the other resources you have in your setting. It may be that they want to take their favourite toy into the space. It is important that they are given free choice and that you do not try to restrict or engineer the play to what you think they should play with.

5 Carry out a narrative observation where you record what the children are doing in their play. Your observation should take the format of a 'story', either in the moment or as soon afterwards as possible, and you should try to capture and focus on what the children are doing with each other and with the resources they have chosen.

6 Decide on how long you will observe the children; remember that the longer you observe the more time it will take to write up your observation.

7 The more children you have in the space the more complicated your observation will become. In this situation you might decide to focus on one or two children in your observation.

8 Try to write down what you see without judging or interpreting the children's actions or behaviour. For example, 'Jasmine sits on the floor, putting cotton reels into an empty sweet tin' rather than 'Jasmine is enjoying heuristic play'.

9 When you complete your observation you may find it useful to have certain key words or 'prompts' about the resources, space, verbal or non-verbal communication in order to help you keep focussed.

Part 2

10 Once you have completed your observation you will need to analyse it in terms of how children are being creative in the space, how they are developing creative behaviours, and how they are developing their play and creativity between them.

11 The following questions will help you to focus and develop your thinking.

- How are the children involved in problem solving?

- Can you recognise children engaging in possibility thinking?

- Are the children playing as individuals or co-constructing their play together?

- How are the children taking risks with the resources and space?

- How might the children be representing their thinking through their play choices?

- How are children using their imagination and their skills in experimenting and exploring curiosity?

12 Share your analysis and thoughts with your colleagues, identifying from the observation and subsequent reflection if you think children engaged in this activity demonstrated creativity and how far this is a typical representation of what happens in your setting.

Question to consider

- *Can children engage in a creative process without the play resulting in an end product?*

Children are able to demonstrate creative ways of being and ways of being in action through play. The process of creativity involves children being risk takers, engaging in possibility thinking and problem solving. There may be an end product to this process as children assume different roles and through the context of play co-construct an outcome or conclusion to their play. The process of play and creativity enables children to take on different roles which can then be explored in different play situations and supports their creative potential. You can also take on a creative way of being to facilitate this process and recognise the end product that the children have created. However, it is important that you do not try to control creativity any more than you try to control play. The emerging processes that occur within the interconnectedness of creativity and play ensure that there is potential for rich learning opportunities which can be extended in other contexts. Crucially, children must have the time and space to develop their play and not be made aware of the end product which may then begin to dominate what they are doing. It is your job to identify the outcome or product and decide on how to capitalise on it, arguably by planning more play opportunities.

Summary

This chapter has focussed on the process or product elements of creativity. It has examined the ambiguity placed on the idea of originality in developing creative products and has considered the role of the practitioner in supporting children by establishing creative ways of thinking and doing. Possibility thinking was considered in relation to your role in asking 'What If' questions to facilitate a creative process that could support further play and learning opportunities where creative dispositions can be developed. Consequently creativity is not considered in isolation but is reflected in children's unique qualities, the relationships they build, and in how the environment facilitates creative experiences. The flexibility required to establish these connections is centred on understanding children's perspectives and remaining child centred via play opportunities which identify ways in which an ethos of creative learning can be supported.

12

The need to measure play?

Natalie Canning

Chapter Objectives

This chapter explores the importance placed on play as a process of learning. It examines the balance between the expectations and value practitioners place on play and how this translates in practice in terms of recognising the contribution play makes to a process of learning and development or seeing play as something that has to be judged and measured against pre-defined outcomes. It explores the impact of children's play experiences based on practitioners' knowledge and understanding and their ability to recognise the significance of child-initiated and holistic play. It also emphasises the role of play as part of effective learning and reflection as a process to support effective practice.

Making judgements about play

When practitioners observe play they make judgements and interpretations about what children are doing, the skills they are practising, the dispositions and ways of being in action that they are demonstrating. These judgements are based on individual interpretations of the play situation and knowledge of the child, but unless you are a child taking part in that particular play you cannot know for sure if your interpretation is accurate about what the child is thinking or the motivation behind the play. Indeed even the child can find it difficult to articulate when asked about this in Circle Time sessions. The process of play when it is child initiated does not focus on an end product or outcome unless this is the child's motivation. The freedom and flexibility within child-led play mean that the process and experience that the child engages in are more important. Does this need to be measured against criteria of what children can and cannot do? Do you need to use the 'development matters' of the six areas of learning in the EYFS as criteria to measure children's processes of engagement in play? Hughes (2001) has argued that children need time and space to be children, away from adult intervention, where they are not judged or expected to achieve. It is their 'time out' and although when children engage in play they may demonstrate learning or the development of a skill, practitioners do not need to measure this because children are already overwhelmed with formal assessments which can more accurately record the achievement of an outcome or produce an end product. In contrast if you can make assessments and judgements of the six areas of learning from children's play then why not? Linfield et al. (2008) argues that if you can do this without interfering with children's play then you can measure the skills that children demonstrate in play through observation. However, consideration needs to be given as to what you understand the term 'measurement' to mean. For example, what are you measuring?

- Perhaps children's ability to play?

- Are you measuring play or are you identifying learning through play?

- Do you believe that these are one in the same thing?

- Are you measuring quality of experience through evaluation?

- Does measuring play have any value?

- Are your measurements 'valid' if they are your individual interpretation of the situation?

The term 'measurement' suggests assessment, which equates with some sort of criteria against which to measure, and the EYFS offers 'development matters' to do this. It states 'the learning and development sections are split into four columns that represent the ongoing cycle of thinking about development and assessing children's progress' (DCSF, 2008: 11), meaning perhaps that 'development matters' should be seen as a process. The practice guidance states in bold that it should not be used as a checklist, but in practice it can often be seen in this way by how any observation, assessment or planning is organised in settings. The EYFS represents one interpretation of how to approach play and how to construct meaning from what you observe in practice. How you interpret the EYFS and the value you place on measurement are both something you need to reflect upon in order to identify where the rationale for your approach comes from.

The expectations of play

Exploring play through the different principles of the EYFS demonstrates the diverse nature and ambiguity of how it is socially constructed, implemented, valued, and assessed (Sutton Smith, 1997). For example, the way in which practitioners make connections between the four principles and how this translates into practice is different in individual settings and relies on how holistic development is viewed. The way in which children access play in your setting will depend on practitioner's expectations of the significance of it in supporting children's development. Play can underpin children's learning but it is practitioners who have to facilitate this process. If practitioners' expectations are too high play becomes outcome driven, focussing on an end product or 'proof' that children have learnt something, and arguably it is then no longer play. If expectations are low then practitioners may miss future opportunities to build on children's interests through informed planning.

The multi-faceted nature of play means that both you and your setting could identify specific examples of play to support children's development. In terms of facilitating this you may choose to adopt different approaches, i.e. at one end of the scale you may use a structured activity which is adult directed and based on pre-defined learning outcomes. This could still be argued as containing elements of play because it might have characteristics of exploration and problem solving for example. At the other end of the scale child-initiated play, where a child leads play without input from an adult and where they decide on the content, space, resources and any outcomes, is perhaps a more authentic perspective of play because children are self-motivated enough to be involved and are following their own interests. In between there will be variations on the amount of support and direction practitioners will give to children and whether this is considered play depends on your definition and underpinning values. However, from whichever perspective you advocate an accepted argument will be that children learn through play, that they experiment and problem solve based on their own experiences. The more difficult question is – do you need to assess learning that occurs through play? Linfield et al. (2008) provides a useful view on this question and sees play as a rich source of assessment opportunities, but what you choose to assess and more importantly how you assess will be based on your own beliefs about the value of play for children and the setting's approach to play. Alternatively, Hughes (2001: 254) argues that we should see play for play's sake as a human right and a human need. He argues children should have ownership of their play, for their own agenda rather than any assessment strategy or criteria.

Samuelsson and Johansson (2006) reviewed the approach to play in Swedish preschools where play had been seen as something to be protected from adult intervention where children could experience freedom. They considered that children engaged in their own motivation to maintain concentration, enthusiasm and learning through trial and error did not need adults to be involved in play. Sweden has now moved towards play being integrated into more formal learning processes. This relies on the practitioner recognising a balance in the process of play and the pedagogical interests of learning. In the case study, Jenny as practitioner demonstrated how she had intuitive capabilities to do this. The children were sufficiently confident to ask for her help and she was able to join in with their play by being aware that they needed to stay in control and so she followed their directions and cues. By her actions she supported their social development and dynamics within the group because she was allowing the children's relationships to evolve without intervention. This supported a child-centred approach to their learning and development. In their imaginary play the children were communicating via speaking and listening. They were demonstrating that they could sustain this using an abstract thought process (going to the moon) and express their emotions within this context. When they were on the spaceship Katie called out to Jenny that she was scared. This provided Jenny with an opportunity to support Katie, without detracting from the play situation and also allowed Jess a way to connect with her peer. Together they supported Katie in her emotional response, but were also effective in maintaining her imagination of going to the moon. Jenny had become part of the play, being able to support the children in their play experience through subtle and sensitive pedagogy. Jenny was also engaged in an authentic assessment of the children's responses, engagement and needs, reflecting in action, to respond appropriately to the play but with the potential for reflection on action after the play had concluded. She was open to using the potential of the situation to inform her practice in the moment of the play.

Pedagogy in play

The term 'pedagogy' is understood as the practice or art of teaching (Siraj-Blatchford, 2004). The DCSF (2009c: 4) views play as part of a pedagogical strategy for learning, placing an emphasis on 'playful approaches for successful outcomes'. As a practitioner within the daily routine of your setting you need to decide what you expect from play in different situations and different contexts and how pedagogy fits into this process. This means understanding the factors that support play and how your involvement will influence how children act and react. The DCSF (2009c: 6) argues that 'practitioners have a key role in building the right conditions for learning', because for learning to develop children need to feel safe and secure, confident and valued, listened to and respected. These qualities are inherent in the four principles of the EYFS but more importantly need to be transferred into your everyday practice. This should emerge through how you *approach* your practice or pedagogy. It is also reliant upon your *attitude* towards pedagogy in relation to how you support children to become independent learners. Siraj-Blatchford (2004) discusses how 'framing' pedagogy is important. This relates to how you plan and create situations for play opportunities, such as having relevant resources which can support a particular theme children have been showing interest in and then how you facilitate children's play and learning though a balance of child-initiated and then more formal practitioner-led activities which can extend children's learning.

Whitebread (2008) argues that it is important to support children in becoming independent and self-regulated learners in order that they can be confident in taking the initiative. Play provides opportunities for children to do this because they are self-motivated to participate. Even if there are rules in the play and a possibility of rejection or failure most children will take the chance to be involved, because they want to be part of what other children are experiencing and enjoying. This not only develops children's understanding of their emotions but also provides them with opportunities to take risks and challenges. It is important to reflect on your practice and consider if the pedagogy you undertake does provide these opportunities for children. One way of thinking about this is to consider when (if at all) you involve children in your setting to plan what they want to do. By doing this you not only ensure you reflect the interests and motivations of the children in your care, you also demonstrate that you are listening to their voices, taking into consideration their opinions, and in the process you are building up their trust and respect. Whitebread (2008) would suggest that over-planned or directed pedagogy gives the impression that areas of learning are covered, but that this approach is ineffective in promoting learning in young children. He suggests that it does not help them to develop the ability or confidence to become independent learners. Pedagogy in play should allow children to take some responsibility for their own learning. This will create not only high quality play, but also high quality practice.

Holistic development

Linfield et al. (2008) believes that effective planning and observation will naturally reveal opportunities for assessment. This places an importance on holistic development within play where observations can concentrate on the processes children engage in rather than on looking for a skill or competency-based outcome. However, it is not enough to make observations and rely on a tick sheet mentality to make judgements against the six areas of learning. Your understanding and analysis of holistic development are vital in ensuring that a play environment will support children's self-initiated learning within meaningful contexts. The play in the case study provided the children with experiences to help them develop a positive sense of both themselves and others. They were able to demonstrate their creative abilities and spontaneous solutions to problems that the 'going to the moon' scenario generated. In their decision to participate the children showed their interest and confidence in linking with others, providing extended opportunities for them to experience sharing an imaginative way of being. Bailey (2002) suggests that this is a natural disposition for children in that they are not usually afraid to 'have a go'. He argues that this is because children are unaware of social consequences at a young age and therefore find it easy to display open communication and co-operation. It is also because children feel safe and secure within a play context and an environment which accepts imperfection, celebrates diversity, and values them for their contribution. In doing this they are developing skills to interpret not only each other's role within the play, but also the emotional role they are able to support while remaining in the 'going to the moon' context. The play provides clear evidence of the children self-perpetuating 'a unique child' as they begin to negotiate relationships, display emotions, and develop confidence and self-assurance.

Smidt (2005: 20) identifies that an assessment of children's learning should be dynamic and not static. She suggests that it is the 'process of gathering together a body of evidence to help one make decisions about what a child knows and can do at a particular point in time'. Play is a way whereby 'evidence' can be collected through observations – however turning that evidence into assessment, judgements about play and an analysis of play contexts is reliant on practitioners' knowledge and understanding. White et al. (2009: 24) argues that 'where assessment is seen as an integral part of the curriculum, adults need to be attuned to the child as a learner within the context of play'. Adopting this approach relies again on the value you place on play and how much you trust that the process of play will generate 'evidence' for an assessment. Children's play can reflect the cultural and philosophical views of your setting, so if you are not 'tuned into' children's play or holistic development then the likelihood is that you will not be able to assess children using this process. However, the EYFS does not make focussing on holistic development easy. It associates high quality early years provision with 'measurements of children's progression and achievement' and 'accurate record keeping including information on children's learning progress' (DCSF, 2008e: 8/10). The Office for Standards in Education (Ofsted) also uses these parameters for their inspections of early years settings.

Measuring play through observation

The chapter so far has asked you to recognise that analysing play situations children engage in is dependent upon the practitioners' level of knowledge and understanding about child development. How they use and interpret that knowledge may lead them to view what they see happening in a completely different way. It is the *interpretation* of play which leads to an assessment and judgement being made about children's learning. It is the *assessment* of learning which leads to practitioners measuring the impact and importance of play. If the interpretation of play is limited because of a lack of time, understanding or knowledge about the possibilities play can generate for children's learning, then the value that practitioners place on play is less significant than the value they place on more formal learning opportunities. For example, a practitioner with a limited knowledge of play may only recognise social and imaginative play when they observe a scenario similar to the case study in their setting. The value of the play narrative that the children develop may then not be seen as so significant because it is not being analysed in the same way. Jenny, the practitioner in the case study, shared how observation, planning and assessment were organised in her setting:

> Our setting's policy is to do two long observations per term on each child. One focusses on child-initiated play and one is carried out during an adult-initiated activity. Our manager decided on this approach because we get a more rounded picture of the child rather than 'snapshots' of their achievements, so observations form a major part of planning in our setting. We keep brief progress notes of the children's interests on a daily basis and these allow us to see how they develop over a period of time. The day-to-day progress notes of anything significant are shared with everyone at the end of the day and we are all employed an extra hour each day to discuss and review the daily activities and to plan for the next day and week ahead. The key person for individual children does the

'next steps' planning but we are all used to sharing our observations with other members of staff, working collaboratively in the interests of each child. (Interview, September, 2009)

Fisher (2008) agrees that collaborative reflection on practice can support observation, assessment, and the planning of children's play. She argues that practitioners need time not only to develop their skill in observing children, but also to reflect on their practice and the judgements they make against children's learning and development. Consequently, by making more detailed observations you are making sense of what is happening, how the setting's environment and your relationships with children support this, and the impact this has for individual children. When children are engaged in child-initiated play you may not always identify their learning intentions. It is sometimes only by reflecting on observations that you can look at your actions and skills as well as the child's reaction. This may involve re-reading notes and having discussions with colleagues which could allow what you have observed to become clearer.

In the case study Jenny reflected that she believed that she had applied her knowledge and understanding of children's interactions to how she stood back from intervening between John and Ben in their disagreement over who should be captain. John quickly assumed control over the situation by establishing a hierarchy and avoided conflict by appointing Ben as his 'deputy'. He understood that Ben also wanted to be in charge and so skilfully offered him another role. He used statements to assert himself, but combined these with 'ok?' questions to keep Ben on his side. Jenny allowed this situation to continue, mindful that Bailey (2002) suggests that children will use communication to manipulate situations to their own advantage. John possessesed the first skills in recognising that he could get his own way by encouraging Ben into a supporting role. The other children accepted him in this role, maybe because of the already established friendships, his assertive qualities without becoming 'bossy', and his ability to support the other children to make their own decisions. Jenny recognised that there were elements of distributed leadership in the play where each child was able to make choices and express their opinion without being pressured to conform. For example, Ben had the idea of getting a space helmet from the scrap materials, but he didn't place this expectation on the other children. Jenny reflected that he was confident enough to express his own ideas, which while taken up by the others, did not rely on them to follow suit. He asserted himself, rather than posing a question or suggestion to them. Jenny acknowledged that this provided an insight into the complex relationships children have with each other. Lofdahl (2006: 86) states that play is 'the arena where children create and maintain positions in their peer group'. She suggests that the relationships children develop through play influence their attitudes and values and that play actions and negotiations about role characters in play influence and reflect the reality of children. By not intervening in this exchange Jenny demonstrated how play can support children in their own learning and how she could recognise this from her observation and critical analysis of the situation.

Observing, listening, and interpreting

Rogoff (1990) provides an analogy of looking at play through three different lenses, supplying researchers with a structure similar to that of Bronfenbrenner (1979). Her research supports the exploration of play through:

- the perspective of the individual child;

- the child as part of a network of relationships and the wider community;

- the child positioned within societal values and associated practices that impact on the way in which play is viewed.

In considering these lenses in terms of reflecting on play the first lens relates to seeing the child's unique qualities, assessing who they are and not necessarily what they know. In the case study, Jenny was able to identify developments in Katie's emotional literacy based on her existing knowledge of how Katie had responded in other play situations. For example, at one point Katie had reached out to Jenny and said that she was scared. Jenny reflected that this was unusual for Katie as she often concealed her emotions:

> Katie was able to express that she was scared but did this whilst staying in character as an astronaut. This demonstrated that she was able to link with me for support and guidance and use language to share her feelings, experiences, and thoughts. She was also able to explore play and seek meaning in her experiences through participating in play with the other children and continuing to play, even though she reached out and shouted over the other children making whooshing noises that she was scared. (Interview, September 2009).

From this child/adult interaction contained within the play Jenny was able to see what was significant for Katie based on her knowledge of previous play experiences. She could use what had happened in this play situation to build on a positive relationship and apply it to planning for future play encounters with Katie. Jenny could also share what happened in the play with her colleagues so they could further support Katie's emotional literacy in different play opportunities – as she was integral to the social relationships developed within the play in the case study. This is the second lens, where assessing positive relationships and enabling environments form the basis for participation and learning in play. In the case study the play environment was successful in providing opportunities for the play to evolve from role play to eventually becoming symbolic pretend play. Initially the children were situated within a role play area. Ben and John were pretending to book a holiday while Jess was packing a toy suitcase. Hughes (2006) defines role play as an attempt by children to engage in an imitation of other people, through their voice, mannerisms, dress or actions. Bailey (2002) argues that pretence is a prerequisite for symbolic representation, i.e. that a child has the ability to adopt and maintain a pretend 'state' before they can use everyday objects to symbolise something else which is meaningful to them in their play. Therefore the role play area supports the development of children's imagination by offering opportunities to explore different scenarios and to put themselves in the place of others. Nevertheless, these areas need to be carefully constructed in order for them to contain open-ended materials for children to develop their capacity for imagination.

Assessing the case study through the third lens reveals the way in which knowledge and understanding of the value of play need to be central to everyone in the setting. The 'going to the moon' play was interrupted by another practitioner, Rachel, announcing snack time and the play was almost immediately lost. The creativity and imaginative processes built and sustained by the children quickly disappeared to be replaced by the rules and time frames of the preschool. The children in this situation conformed to the socially constructed boundaries of the setting that were in place for the organisation of the day. This provided a message to children that the play and learning processes they were involved in were not as important as the structure of the preschool. They learnt that time frames were adult controlled and directed and that the overall environment was inflexible to other play opportunities. In considering Rogoff's lenses, perhaps the most significant in terms of the role of the practitioner in leading effective practice is that which focusses on the child's experience in the setting. The setting in the case study supported a reflective dialogue to try to ensure the child's voice could be acknowledged through planning and observations. Rachel's intervention in the play was reflected upon at the end of the day where the team discussed the significance of daily routines in relation to purposeful play. In assessing children's learning through play the team reflected on how they could apply a unified approach to play to ensure that mixed messages were not sent via different practitioners to the children.

Continuous Professional Development Activity

This activity identifies the holistic nature of play and supports your reflection on how you can analyse and subsequently assess play. The observation grid of 'going to the moon' (Table 12.1) provides an overview of the processes that are happening at each stage in the case study. This is considered in a visual representation and is interpreted through the four principles of the EYFS. The processes that the children display in their play sometimes overlap, but they still provide a 'best fit' to demonstrate the wealth of evidence and assessment that can be collected from one observation.

Analysing children's play narratives

Aims

- To consider how you analyse your observations of children in your setting.

- To explore whether your assessment of children's play is process driven or outcome led.

- To reflect on how you interpret children's play and your observations to make assessments of the skills they are developing.

 Activity

1 Look at the grid in Table 12.1 which outlines a play narrative and provides analysis of the case study in relation to the four principles of the EYFS.

2 Think of an example of play from your own practice or use the observation you made in the CPD activity for Chapter 11.

3 Break down your observation into sections so you can analyse each part. Try to represent each section of your observation with a picture or diagram of what is happening. The top row of the grid is an example of what is happening in the case study.

4 Once you are happy with your visual representation analyse each section in relation to the four principles of the EYFS.

5 Consider how you are interpreting each principle in relation to the different sections of your observation. How objective is your analysis?

6 When you have completed your grid reflect on whether you have made an assessment of the children in the observation.

7 Within your analysis consider if you have focussed on a developing process within the play observation or if any end products/outcomes have emerged from what you have written.

8 Discuss with your colleagues how this activity may influence or change the way you observe and assess children in your setting.

Table 12.1 'Going to the moon' play narrative

The Play Narrative - visual representation of the story	Travel Shop	Transition	To the Moon	Responding and Extending	In the Space Ship	Interruption
Unique Child	• Child initiated • Articulation of different interests through actions and words	• Choice and responses • Decision making	• Establishing a hierarchy • Distributed leadership	• Individual identity, expression and need	• Role of individual in play continues	• Not recognised
Positive Relationships	• Awareness of each other • Response to and communication of interests • Intention to play together	• Child led interaction • Respect (open questioning) • Boundaries and personal understanding of others	• Supportive • Active listening • Valued • Child/child interaction	• Adult/child interaction • Respect • Connection within the play • Mutual participation	• Hierarchy is maintained • Child centred • Child and adult interaction is mutually appreciated	• Ended • Lack of respect for creativity • Valueless
Enabling Environments	• Props used to support imagination • Variety of play opportunities • Adult free	• Flexible • Enough space	• Enables symbolic pretend play	• Maintains symbolic pretend play	• Maintains symbolic pretend play	• Destroyed • Inflexible (snack time)
Learning and Development	• Interaction • Awareness of the different contexts	• Possibility thinking • Creativity • Imagination • Language and thought	• Imagination • Actions • Language • Potential schema	• Jenny is scaffolding thinking through different modes of representation • Co-construction	• Extending thought within the role play • Stimulating responses	• Socially constructed boundaries • Time frames • Rules

Question to consider

- *Have you measured play?*

In considering your observation and analysis of the four principles organised in your grid you may consider that you have measured play by making judgements about what happened in the play you observed and categorising what the children did under certain principles. It is now important to consider what you are going to do with your analysis and whether making the assessment will have any meaningful implications for future practice. It is also important to consider the impact on your professional development as well as the implications of measuring play for the children. In the case study Jenny was skilful in her pedagogical approach, recognising where she could extend specific learning opportunities in a meaningful way. For example, she counted down the launch of the spaceship and was aware that by doing this she was encouraging the children to a) join in and b) make meaningful connections between numbers and their use in context. You could argue that she was measuring the children's ability to count through play, yet her assessment was not obvious to the children. The play remained grounded in the child/child relationships and interactions, but Jenny was sensitively supporting these in her responses to the children's requests and her ability to stay within the play scenario. She therefore built a capacity for the children to extend their own thought which would stimulates their responses and actions.

☐ Summary

This chapter has explored the implications of play as process-driven practice and where assessment sits within it. It has recognised that an essential element to the extent to which you measure play is your values and beliefs about the purpose and motivation for play in your setting. The chapter has argued for a balance and focus on holistic development to recognise the four principles of the EYFS but not to rely on the areas of learning as outcome focussed. It has recognised that if you use a sophisticated tool for observation then you will get a more sophisticated response which can contribute to your knowledge and understanding, values and beliefs about what children are doing when they play. The way in which the EYFS is organised compels you to assess play, but it is important to recognise your role within this, enabling the child to take the lead and reflect upon how you interpret what you observe. These decisions will then impact upon the opportunities you provide for play and how you use the EYFS to underpin play-based practice.

Conclusion

Natalie Canning

Different perspectives of play have been identified and analysed in this text to support you in understanding play both in your practice and in the context of your setting. The EYFS has been explored in relation to four case studies involving children, practitioners, parents and the wider community. The chapters have related to the four principles of the EYFS – A Unique Child, Positive Relationships, Enabling Environments, Learning and Development. Within these you have had the opportunity to reflect on different views about play, what play means for practice, what it means for you and, importantly, the time necessary to reflect on the impact of play for children and their development.

In working with children, play should be the starting point for everything you do. It informs you about children's qualities, their expressions of interest, their likes and dislikes, how they explore and imagine, and how they learn. Play asks you to question how much involvement you should have and who has ownership of play situations. Play is a journey of discovery for children. You can be part of that journey, but it is important not to hijack the route children take through play to new experiences and exploration. In trusting children on their journey you create a capacity for risk taking, challenge and achievement – all essential ingredients for early childhood and holistic practice.

From considering the perspective of the chapters in the book I hope that you will examine the experiences you offer children through play, your own values about the importance of play, and how you approach play in practice. The ambiguity of the EYFS means that you can have some flexibility in finding your own way to delivering quality play experiences and essentially this text hopes that you will do this based on informed decisions about the significance of play for children's immediate development, their disposition towards lifelong learning, and providing them with the chance for positive play memories.

175

References

11 Million and Play England (2008) *Fun and Freedom: What children say about play in a sample of play strategy consultations*. London: National Children's Bureau and 11 Million.

Ainsworth, M. (1969) 'Object relations, dependency and attachment; a theoretical review of the infant mother relationship', *Child Development*, 40(4): 969–1045.

Anning, A. and Edwards, A. (2010) 'Young children as learners', in L. Miller, C. Cable and G. Goodliff (eds), *Supporting Children's Learning in the Early Years* (2nd edition). London: David Fulton.

Arnold, C. (2003) *Observing Harry*. Maidenhead: Open University Press.

Athey, C. (1990) *Extending Thought in Young Children: A parent teacher partnership*. London: Paul Chapman.

Bailey, R. (2002) 'Playing social chess: children's play and social intelligence', *Early Years*, 22(2): 163–173.

Bandura, A. (1962) 'Social learning through imitation', in M.R. Jones (ed.), *Nebraska Symposium on Motivation*. Chicago: University of Chicago Press.

Barnes, C. (2000) 'The social model of disability: a sociological phenomenon ignored by sociologists?', in T. Shakespeare (ed.), *The Disability Reader: Social science perspectives*. London: Continuum.

Bauman, Z. and May, T. (2001) *Thinking Sociologically* (2nd edition). Oxford: Blackwell.

Bion, W. (1962) *Learning from Experience*. London: Heinemann.

Blackmore, S. and Frith, U. (2007) *The Learning Brain: Lessons for education*. Oxford: Blackwell.

Booth, T., Ainscow, M. and Kingston, D. (2006) *Index for Inclusion: Developing play, learning and participation in early years and childcare*. London: Centre for Studies on Inclusive Education.

Bowlby, J. (1988) *A Secure Base*. London: Routledge.

Brisenden, S. (2000) 'Independent living and the medical model of disability', in T. Shakespeare (ed.), *The Disability Reader: Social science perspectives*. London: Continuum.

Broadhead, P. (2004) *Early Years Play and Learning Developing Social Skills and Co-operation*. London: RoutledgeFalmer.

Broadhead, P. (2006) 'Developing an understanding of young children's learning through play: the place of observation, interaction and reflection', *British Educational Research Journal*, 32(2): 191–207.

Bronfenbrenner, U. (1979) *The Ecology of Human Development: Experiments by nature and design*. Cambridge, MA: Harvard University Press.

Brown, F. (2003) 'Compound flexibility', in F. Brown (ed.), *Playwork: Theory into practice*. Maidenhead: Open University Press.

Bruce, T. (2001) *Learning through Play: Babies, toddlers and the foundation years.* London: Hodder Arnold.

Bruce, T. (2005) *Early Childhood Education* (3rd edition). London: Hodder Arnold.

Bruner, J.S. (1966) *Towards a Theory of Instruction.* Cambridge, MA: Harvard University Press.

Bruner, J.S. (1972) 'The nature and uses of immaturity', *American Psychologist,* 27(1): 1–28.

Burke, C. (2008) 'Play in focus: children's visual voice in participative research', in P. Thomson (ed.), *Doing Visual Research with Children and Young People.* London: Routledge.

Burnard, P., Craft, A. and Cremin, T. (2006) 'Documenting "possibility thinking": a journey of collaborative enquiry', *International Journal of Early Years Education,* 14(3): 243–262.

Callan, S. and Morrall, A. (2009) 'Working with parents', in A. Robins, and S. Callan (eds), *Managing Early Years Settings.* London: SAGE.

Canning, N. (2007) 'Children's empowerment in play', *European Early Childhood Education Research Journal,* 15(2): 227–236.

Cassidy, J., Parke, R., Butkovsky, L. and Braungart, J. (1992) 'Family–peer connections: the roles of emotional expressiveness within the family and children's understanding of emotions', *Child Development,* 63(3): 603–618.

Chappell, A.L. (2000) 'Still out in the cold: people with learning difficulties and the social model of disability', in T. Shakespeare (ed.), *The Disability Reader: Social science perspectives.* London: Continuum.

Clark, A. and Moss, P. (2001) *Listening to Young Children: The Mosaic approach.* London: National Children's Bureau.

Coe, C., Gibson, A., Spencer, N. and Stuttaford, M. (2008) 'SureStart: Voices of the "hard to reach"', *Childcare and Health Development Journal,* 34(4): 447–453.

Cohen, D. and MacKeith, S.A. (1991) *The Development of Imagination: The private worlds of childhood.* London: Routledge.

Craft, A. (2000) *Creativity across the Primary Curriculum: Framing and developing practice.* London: Routledge.

Craft, A. (2001) 'Little c creativity', in A. Craft, B. Jeffrey and M. Liebling (eds), *Creativity in Education.* London, Continuum.

Craft, A. (2003) 'The limits to creative education', *British Journal of Educational Studies,* 51(2): 113–127.

Csikszentmihalyi, M. (1997) *Creativity: Flow and the psychology of discovery and invention.* New York: Harper Perennial.

de Kruif, R., McWilliam, R., Ridley, S. and Wakely, M. (2000) 'Classification of teachers' interaction behaviours in early childhood classrooms', *Early Childhood Research Quarterly,* 15(2): 247–268.

Denham, S., McKinley, M., Couchould, E. and Holt, R. (1990) 'Emotional and behavioural predictors of preschool peer ratings', *Child Development,* 61(6): 1145–1152.

Department for Children, Schools and Families (DCSF) (2007a) *All about … Working with Parents – Practice guidance for the Early Years Foundation Stage.* Nottingham: DCSF.

Department for Children, Schools and Families (DCSF) (2007b) *Every Parent Matters.* Nottingham: DCSF.

Department for Children, Schools and Families (DCSF) (2007c) *The Children's Plan: Building Brighter Futures.* London: The Stationery Office.

Department for Children, Schools and Families (DCSF) (2008a) *Card 1.1 EYFS A Unique Child: Child development – principle into practice.* Nottingham, DCSF.

Department for Children, Schools and Families (DCSF) (2008b) *Card 3.1 Enabling*

Environments: Observation, assessment and planning – principle into practice. Nottingham, DCSF.

Department for Children, Schools and Families (DCSF) (2008c) *Card 3.3 EYFS Enabling Environments: The learning environment – principle into practice.* Nottingham, DCSF.

Department for Children, Schools and Families (DCSF) (2008d) *Card 4.3 EYFS Learning and Development: Creativity and critical thinking – principle into practice.* Nottingham, DCSF.

Department for Children, Schools and Families (DCSF) (2008e) *Practice Guidance for the Early Years Foundation Stage.* Nottingham: DFES.

Department for Children, Schools and Families (DCSF) (2008f) *Statutory Framework for the Early Years Foundation Stage.* Nottingham: DCSF.

Department for Children, Schools and Families (DCSF) (2008g) *Early Years Quality Support Improvement Programme.* Nottingham: DCSF.

Department for Children Schools and Families (DCSF) (2008h) *The National Strategies: Early Years Quality Improvement Support Programme (EYQISP).* Nottingham: DCSF.

Department for Children, Schools and Families (DCSF) (2009a) *Next Steps for Early Learning and Childcare: Building on the 10 year strategy.* Nottingham: DCSF.

Department for Children, Schools and Families (DCSF) (2009b) 'SureStart Children Centre Principles', available at http://www.dcsf.gov.uk/everychildmatters/earlyyears/surestart/thesurestartprinciples/principles/ (last accessed 11.12.09).

Department for Children, Schools and Families (DCSF) (2009c) *Learning, Playing and Interacting: Good practice in the Early Years Foundation Stage.* Nottingham: DCSF.

Department for Children, Schools and Families (DCSF) and Department of Health (DoH) (2008) *Aiming Higher for Disabled Children: Delivering the core offer standard.* Nottingham: DCSF.

Department for Children, Schools and Families (DCSF), Department of Health (DoH) and Department for Work and Pensions (DWP) (2006) *Raising Standards – Improving Outcomes Statutory Guidance Early Years outcomes Duty Childcare Act 2006.* Nottingham: DCSF.

Department for Education and Skills (DfES) (2002) *Birth to Three Matters: A framework to support children in their earliest years.* London: DfES.

Department for Education and Skills (DfES) (2004) *Every Child Matters: Change for Children.* Nottingham: DfES.

Department for Education and Skills (DfES) (2005a) *Implementing the DDA: Improving access: Early Years.* London: HMSO.

Department for Education and Skills (DfES) (2005b) 'The KEEP project (Key Elements of Effective Practice)'. Available at http://www.niched.org/docs/key%20elements%20of%20effective%20practice%20KEEP.pdf (last accessed 10.12.09).

Department for Education and Skills (DfES) (2005c) *Common Core of Skills and Knowledge for the Children's Workforce.* Nottingham: DfES.

Department of Health (DoH) (2004) 'Choosing health: making healthy choices easier', Public Health White paper.

Desforges, C. and Abouchaar, A. (2003) *The Impact of Parental Involvement, Parental Support and Family Education on Pupil Achievement and Adjustment: A literature review: research report RR433.* London: DfES. Available online at http://www.dfes.gov.uk/research/data/uploadfiles/RR433.pdf

Donaldson, M. (1978) *Children's Minds.* London: Fontana.

Donaldson, M. (1992) *Human Minds: An exploration.* London: Penguin.

Dudek, M. (2000) *Architecture of Schools: The new learning environments.* Boston, MA: Architectural.

Duffy, B. (2006) *Supporting Creativity and Imagination in the Early Years* (2nd edition). Maidenhead: Open University Press.

Dunn, J. (1984) *Sisters and Brothers*. London: Fontana.

Dunn, J. (1986) 'Children in a family world', in M. Richards and P. Light (eds), *Children of Social Worlds: Development in a social context*. Cambridge: Polity.

Dunn, J. (1993) *Young Children's Close Relationships Beyond Attachment*. London: SAGE.

Edgington, M. (2002) 'High levels of achievement for young children', in J. Fisher (ed.), *The Foundations of Learning*. Maidenhead: Open University Press.

Else, P. and Sturrock, G. (2000) *Therapeutic Playwork Reader One 1995–2000*. Eastleigh: Common Threads.

Erikson, E. (1963) *Childhood and Society* (2nd edition). New York: Norton.

Evangelou, M., Sylva, K., Edwards, A. and Smith, T. (2008) *Supporting Parents in Promoting Early Learning*. Nottingham: DCSF and Oxford University.

Fabes, R., Martin, C.L. and Hanish, L. (2003) 'Young children's play qualities in same and other mixed sex peer groups', *Child Development*, 74(3): 921–932.

Fisher, J., (2008) *Starting from the Child* (3rd edition). Maidenhead: OUP/McGraw Hill.

Fisher, R. (2004) 'What is creativity?', in R. Fisher and M. Williams (eds), *Unlocking Creativity: Teaching across the Curriculum*. London: David Fulton.

Fjortoft, I. (2004) 'Landscape as playspace: the effects of natural environments on children's play and motor development', *Children, Youth and Environments* 14(2): 21–44.

Fraiberg, S., Adelson, F. and Shapiro, V. (1975) 'Ghosts in the nursery: a psychoanalytic approach to the problem of impaired infant-mother relationships', *J. Amer. Acad. Child Psychiat*, 14(3): 387–421.

Freire, P. (1970) *Pedagogy of the Oppressed*. New York: Herder and Herder.

Gardner, H. (1997) *Extraordinary Minds: Portraits of exceptional individuals and an examination of our extraordinariness*. New York: Basic.

Gasper, M. (2010) *Multi-agency Working in the Early Years Challenges and Opportunities*. London: SAGE.

Goldschmied, E. and Jackson, S. (2004) *People under Three: Young Children in Day Care* (2nd edition). London: Routledge.

Greene, S. and Hill, M. (2005) 'Researching children's experience: methods and methodological issues', in S. Greene and D. Hogan (eds), *Researching Children's Experiences: Approaches and Methods*. London: SAGE.

Guilbaud, S. (2003) 'The Essence of Play', in F. Brown (ed.), *Playwork: Theory and Practice*. Maidenhead: Open University Press.

Hughes, B. (2001) *Evolutionary Playwork and Reflective Analytic Practice*. London: Routledge.

Hughes, B. (2002) *A Playworker's Taxonomy of Play Types* (2nd edition). London: PlayLink.

Hughes, B. (2006) *Play Types: Speculations and Possibilities*. London: Centre for Playwork Education and Training.

Hughes, F. (1999) *Children, Play and Development* (3rd edition). Boston, MA: Allyn and Bacon.

Hutt, C. (1979) 'Exploration and play', in B. Sutton Smith (ed.), *Play and Learning*. New York: Gardner.

Hyde, B. (2008) *Children and Spirituality: Searching for meaning and connectedness*. London: Jessica Kingsley.

Hyder, T. (2005) *War, Conflict and Play*. Maidenhead: Open University Press.

Jackson, A. (2010) 'Defining and measuring quality in Early Years settings', in M. Reed and N. Canning (eds), *Reflective Practice in the Early Years*. London: SAGE.

Jenkinson, S. (2001) *The Genius of Play: Celebrating the spirit of childhood*. Stroud: Hawthorn.

Kadis, A. (2007) 'The risk factor', *Play Today*, 60(November).

Kalliala, M. (2009) '"Look at me!" Does the adult see the child in a Finnish day care centre?'. Conference paper presented at the *19th European Early Childhood Education Research Association – Diversities in Early Childhood Education*, Strasbourg, 26–29 August.

Karmiloff-Smith, A. (1994) *Baby it's You*. London: Ebury/Random House.

Katz, L. (1993) 'What can we learn from Reggio Emilia?' in C. Edwards, L. Gandini and G. Forman (eds), *The Hundred Languages of Children: The Reggio Emilia approach to early childhood education*. New Jersey: Norwood.

Katz, L. (1994) 'Perspectives on the quality of early childhood programs', *Phi Delta Kappan*, 76(3): 200–205.

Laevers, F. (2000) 'Forward to basics! Deep level learning and the experiential approach', *Early Years*, 20(2): 20–29.

Langsted, O. (1994) 'Looking at quality from the child's perspective', in P. Moss and A. Pence (eds), *Valuing Quality in Early Childhood Services: New approaches to definging quality*. London: Paul Chapman.

Layard, R. and Dunn, J. (2009) *A Good Childhood – Searching for Values in a Competitive Age*. London: Penguin Books and The Children's Society.

Lewis, M. (1997) 'The social determination of play', in B. Sutton-Smith (ed.), *Play and Learning*. New York: Gardner.

Linfield, R., Warwick, P. and Parker, C. (2008) '"I'm putting crosses for the letters I don't know": assessment in the Early Years', in D. Whitebread and P. Coltman (eds), *Teaching and Learning in the Early Years* (3rd edition). London: Routledge.

Lofdahl, A. (2006) 'Grounds for values and attitudes: children's play and peer cultures in pre school', *Journal of Early Childhood Research*, 4(1): 77–88.

Loveless, A. (2005) 'Thinking about creativity: developing ideas, making things happen', in A. Wilson (ed.), *Creativity in Primary Education*. Exeter: Learning Matters.

Lowenfeld, V. and Brittain, L.W. (1987) *Creative and Mental Growth* (8th edititon). New Jersey: Prentice Hall.

Ludvigsen, A., Creegan, C. and Mills, H. (2005) *Let's Play Together: Play and inclusion, evaluation of better play* (Round 3). London: Barnardo's Policy and Research Unit.

MacMahon, L. (1992) *The Handbook of Play Therapy*. London: Routledge.

Malaguzzi, L. (1993) 'For an education based on relationship', *Young Children*, 11: 9–13.

Malaguzzi, L. (1994) 'Your image of the child: where teaching begins', *Childcare Information Exchange*, 3: 52–61.

Maslow, A. (1971) *The Farthest Reaches of Human Nature*. New York: Viking.

Mayall, B. (2002) *Towards a Sociology of Childhood: Thinking from children's lives*. Maidenhead: Open University Press.

McInnes, K. (2007) *A Practitioner's Guide to Interagency Working in Children's Centres: A review of the literature*. London: Barnardo's Policy and Research Unit.

McNaughton, G. (2003) *Shaping Early Childhood*. Maidenhead: Open University Press.

Meade, A. (1995) *Thinking Children and Learning about Schemas*. New Zealand: NZCER.

Meadows, S. (1986) *Understanding Child Development: Psychological perspectives in an interdisciplinary field of enquiry*. London: Hutchinson.

Melhuish, E. (2001) 'The quest for quality in early day care and pre school experience continues', *International Journal of Behavioural Development*, 25(1): 1–6.

Mooney, C.G. (2000) *Theories of Childhood: An introduction to Dewey, Montessori, Erikson, Piaget and Vygotsky*. United States: Redleave.

Moss, P., Brophy, J. and Stratham, J. (2007) 'Parental involvement in playgroups', *Children in Society*, 6(4): 297–316.

Moyles, J. (2005) 'Introduction', in J. Moyles (ed.), *The Excellence of Play* (2nd edition). Maidenhead: Open University Press.

National Advisory Committee on Creative and Cultural Education (NACCCE) (2000) *Creativity and Cultural Education: All Our Futures: A Summary*. London: National Campaign for the Arts.

National Quality Improvement Network (NQIN) (2007) *Quality Improvement Principles: A framework of local authorities and national organisations to improve quality outcomes for children and young people*. London: National Children's Bureau.

Nicholson, S. (1971) 'How not to cheat children: The theory of 'loose parts', *Landscape Architecture Quarterly*, 62(1): 30–35.

Office for Standards in Education, Children's Services and Skills (Ofsted) (2008) *Are You Ready for Your Inspection? A guide to inspections of provision on Ofsted's childcare and early years registers*. London: Ofsted.

Office of Public Sector Information (OPSI) (1996) 'Education Act 1996: Section 312, Part IV Special Educational Needs: Chapter 1 Children with Special Educational Needs', available at http://www.opsi.gov.uk/ACTS/acts1996/ukpga_19960056_en_20 (last accessed 22.12.09).

Office of Public Sector Information (OPSI) (2005) 'Disability Discrimination Act 2005: Section1, Part 1, Disability' , available at http://www.opsi.gov.uk/acts/acts1995/ukpga_19950050_en_2#pt1-l1g1 (last accessed 22.12.09).

Packard, S. (2006) 'Places to play: working together for play friendly public space', *Play England Conference*, Westminster, London, 11 October.

Paley, V.G. (2005) *A Child's Work: The importance of fantasy play*. London: University of Chicago Press.

Parten, M. (1933) 'Social play among pre-school children', *Journal of Abnormal and Social Psychology*, 28(2): 136–147.

Piaget, J. (2001) *The Psychology of Intelligence* (Routledge Classics). Translated by D.E. Berlyne and M. Piercy. London: Routledge.

Play England (2008) *Managing Risk in Play Provision: A position statement*. London: National Children's Bureau.

Prochner, L., Cleghorn, A. and Green, N. (2008) 'Space considerations: materials in the learning environment in three majority world preschool settings', *International Journal of Early Years Education*, 16(3): 189–201.

Qualification and Curriculum Authority (QCA) (2004) *Creativity: Find it, promote it*. London: QCA.

Qvortrup, J., Bardy, M., Sgritta, G. and Wintersberger, H. (eds) (1994) *Childhood Matters*. Vienna: European Centre.

Reddy, V. and Trevarthen, C. (2004) 'What we learn about babies from engaging with their emotions', *Zero to Three*, 24(3): 9–15.

Rinaldi, C. (2005) *In Dialogue with Reggio Emilio: Listening, researching, learning*. London: RoutledgeFalmer.

Robinson, K. (2001) *Out of Our Minds: Learning to be creative*. West Sussex: Capstone.

Robinson, M. (2008) *Child Development from Birth to Eight: A journey through the early years*. Maidenhead: Open University Press.

Rogers, N. (2000) *The Creative Connection: Expressive arts as healing*. Ross-on-Wye: PCCS.

Rogoff, B. (1990) *Apprenticeship in Thinking: Cognitive development in social context.* Oxford: OUP.

Rogoff, B. (2003) *The Cultural Nature of Human Development.* Oxford: OUP.

Royal College of Psychiatrists (2006) 'Spirituality and mental health', available at www.rcpsych.ac.uk/mentalhealthinfo/treatments/spirituality.aspx (last accessed 26.7.09).

Samuelsson, I. and Johansson, E. (2006) 'Play and learning – inseparable dimensions in pre school practice', *Early Child Development and Care,* 176(1): 47–65.

Schön, D. (1987) *Educating the Professional Practitioner.* San Francisco, CA: Jossey-Bass.

Shackell, A., Butler, N., Doyle, P. and Ball, D. (2008) *Design for Play: A guide to creating successful play spaces.* Nottingham: Play England/National Children's Bureau, DCSF.

Siraj-Blatchford, I. (2004) 'Quality teaching in the early years', in A. Anning, J. Cullen and M. Fleer (eds), *Early Childhood Education: Society and culture.* London: SAGE.

Siraj-Blatchford, I. (2007) 'Creativity, communication and collaboration: the identification of pedagogic progression in sustained shared thinking', *Asia-Pacific Journal of Research in Early Childhood Education,* 1(2): 3–24.

Siraj-Blatchford, I. and Sylva, K. (2004) 'Researching pedagogy in English pre-schools', *British Educational Research Journal,* 30(5): 713–730.

Skills Active (2004) 'Playwork principles', available at http://www.skillsactive.com/playwork/principles (last accessed 26.7.09).

Smidt, S. (2005) *Observing, Assessing and Planning for Children in the Early Years.* London: Routledge.

Smidt, S. (2006) *The Developing Child in the 21st Century.* Oxon: Routledge.

Smidt, S. (2009) *Introducing Vygotsky: A guide for practitioners and students in early years education.* London: Routledge.

Smith, P. (2010) *Children and Play.* Oxford: Wiley-Blackwell.

Smith, P., Cowie, H. and Blades, M. (2003) *Understanding Children's Development* (4th edition). London: Blackwell.

Stephenson, A. (2003) 'Physical risk taking: dangerous or endangered?', *Early Years,* 23(1): 35–43.

Sutcliffe, R. (2007) 'Managing risk in play provision', *Play Today,* 60(November).

Sutton Smith, B. (1997) *The Ambiguity of Play.* Cambridge, MA: Harvard University Press.

Sylva, K. and Pugh, G. (2005) 'Transforming the early years in education', *Oxford Review of Education,* 31(1): 11–27.

Thoits, P. (1989) 'The sociology of emotions', *Annual Review of Sociology,* 15: 317–342.

Trevarthen, C. (2004) 'Learning about ourselves, from children: why a growing human brain needs interesting companions', available at http://www.perception-in-action.ed.ac.uk/PDF_s/Colwyn2004.pdf (University of Edinburgh: Perception in Action Publications and last accessed 31.12.09).

Trevarthen, C. (2005) 'First things first: infants make good use of the sympathetic rhythm of imitation, without reason or language', *Journal of Child Psychotherapy,* 31(1): 91–113.

Trevarthen, C. (2009) 'Growth of a meaningful brain: how motives and feelings are shared with companions in a cultural world'. Conference paper presented at *Baby Brains Conference,* London, The School of Infant Mental Health, 16–17 May.

Trevarthen, C., Rodrigues, H., Bjørkvold, J.R., Danon-Boileau, L. and Krantz, G. (2008) 'Valuing creative art in childhood', *Children in Europe: Picture this:*

Young Children in the Arts, 14: 6–9.

Vernon, E. (1989) 'Mary Ainsworth and the development of attachment', *Iris: A Journal about Women*, 21(2): 10–12.

Vygotsky, L.S. (1966) 'Play and its role in the mental development of the child', available at http://www.marxists.org/archive/vygotsky/works/1933/play.htm (last accessed 01.01.10).

Vygotsky, L.S. (1978) *Mind in Society: Development of higher psychological processes*. Harvard: Harvard University Press.

Walkerdine, V. (2004) 'Developmental psychology and the study of childhood', in M.J. Kehily (ed.), *An Introduction to Childhood Studies*. Maidenhead: Open University Press and McGraw-Hill Education.

Waller, T. (2005) 'Modern childhood: contemporary theories and children's lives', in T. Waller (ed.), *An Introduction to Early Childhood: A Multidisciplinary approach*. London: Paul Chapman and SAGE.

Wells, G. (1987) *The Meaning Makers: Children learning language and using language to learn*. London: Heinemann Educational.

Whalen, M. (1995) 'Working toward play: complexity in children's fantasy activities', *Language in Society*, 24(3): 315–348.

Whalley, M. (2007) *Involving Parents in their Children's Learning* (2nd edition). London: SAGE.

White, J., Ellis, F., O'Malley, A., Rockel, J., Stover, S. and Toso, M. (2009) 'Play and learning in Aotearoa, New Zealand, Early Childhood Education', in I. Pramling-Samuelsson and M. Fleer (eds), *Play and Learning in Early Childhood Settings: International Perspectives*. London: Springer.

White, M. and Cameron, R.J. (1987) *Portage Early Education Programme*. Oxford: Heinemann.

Whitebread, D. (2008) 'Young children learning and early years teaching', in D. Whitebread and P. Coltman (eds), *Teaching and Learning in the Early Years* (3rd edition). London: Routledge.

Whitebread, D., Dawkins, R., Bingham, S., Aguda, A. and Hemming, K. (2008) '"Our classroom is like a little cosy house!" Organising the early years classroom to encourage independent learning', in D. Whitebread and P. Coltman (eds), *Teaching and Learning in the Early Years* (3rd edition). London: Routledge.

Winnicott, D. (1971) *Playing and Reality*. London: Routledge.

Wood, E. and Attfield, J. (2005) *Play, Learning and the Early Childhood Curriculum* (2nd edition). London: Paul Chapman.

Wyse, D. and Dowson, P. (2009) *The Really Useful Creativity Book*. London: Routledge.

Index